# THE
# PACIFIC
# COAST
# LEAGUE

# *The Pacific Coast League*

## ONE MAN'S MEMORIES
## 1938 – 1957

by Ken Stadler

MARBEK *Publications*

LOS ANGELES, CALIF.

This edition has been re-set in Palatino, with headings in Akzidenz Grotesk BE.
The book design, cover and illustrations are by Edward A. Rapka

# ACKNOWLEDGMENTS

To my close friend Rich Timmis because of his great love for, and knowledge of, the PCL — I say thanks for giving me the impetus to pen these memories. I deeply appreciate his counsel and contribution.

\* \* \* \*

A special thanks to Clifford Kachline, former Historian of the Baseball Hall of Fame, who graciously and quickly responded to my several burdensome requests. Cliff is currently the Executive Director of the Society for American Baseball Research, of which I am proud to be a member.

\* \* \* \*

I'm grateful to the players who responded to my requests for pictures and autographs. Some of these men I have become personally acquainted with, and they will remain lifelong friends. To those who declined to respond—I respect their wishes.

\* \* \* \*

I wish to express my sincere thanks to Edward Rapka for his outstanding artwork and for accomplishing the many detailed matters necessary to bring about the production of this book.

\* \* \* \*

Finally, thanks to my wife, Mary Ann, for giving so much time in typing and correcting my work. Her job as a phone company secretary has equipped her to be of utmost value to me. Words cannot express my love for and appreciation of her for the countless hours given to this, my first attempt at writing.

*I am pleased to dedicate this book
to Jigger Statz, a wonderful person
and the greatest player in the history
of the Pacific Coast League.*

## ABOUT THE AUTHOR

Ken Stadler is a native Californian and lifetime resident of Santa Monica. Although educated as a Doctor of Chiropractic, he spent over 20 years in the water conditioning industry before retiring in 1980.

I have had the opportunity of being Ken's pastor for the past several years. When I first saw his scrapbook, I knew I had a baseball nut on my hands. From our experiences together, I've realized a wonderful sense of humor and have learned a little bit about the sport he dearly loves.

Although interested in all sports, baseball has been his overwhelming love since childhood. The Pacific Coast League has played a big part in his baseball life.

I'm sure many others, after reading this book, will benefit from his investment and love for the game.

Well, I've said enough. Turn the page and enjoy!

*Wally Johnston*
*Pastor/Freelance Writer*

# CONTENTS

## GILMORE FIELD AND THE HOLLYWOOD STARS

## THE PACIFIC COAST LEAGUE

# FOREWORD

Rich Timmis is a long-time friend who, like me, grew up in Pacific Coast League territory—Berkeley, to be exact. This meant his favorite team was the Oakland Oaks. He was indeed a dedicated fan by its truest definition. As a young man, he played semi-pro ball in the East Bay with the likes of Vada Pinson, Frank Robinson, Jess Gonder and Charlie Beamon. All of these, with the exception of Robinson, played in the PCL. Rich passed up a chance to play pro ball by going into the service. After completing his days in the military, he moved to Southern California, and we became good friends. I rarely, if ever, see him but what we don't get on the subject of baseball. Somewhere along the line we began to throw former PCL player's names around to see if we mutually remembered them. One day the thought crossed my mind: why not have a friendly contest to see which one of us could record, strictly from memory, the most names of players, coaches and managers who were in the Pacific Coast League between the years of 1938 and 1957? I wrote up a challenge and some rules to guide us (see *The Contest*). I remember keeping paper and pencil by my bed and how it would frighten my wife when suddenly a name hit me and I'd jump up, turn on the light and write the player's name down. Billboards, office signs, street names, etc., aided me in my quest.

I tried every method I could think of to assist me. This was not easy, since I've been operating in a somewhat undemanding capacity these past few years. To help keep things straight in my mind, and because recalling these names led to many memories involving the 20 years I have spent as a Coast League fan, I began to write it all down.

Eventually, this book you have before you began to develop. It's divided into two parts. The first portion deals with Gilmore Field and the Hollywood Stars, and the second with the Coast League itself.

There are no chapters, simply headings.

I hope you will enjoy what I recall about those days. I also hope that it will cause former players and fans alike to call to mind the good times we enjoyed in the PCL. Even if you disagree with me on certain points, it matters not. If I have stirred you to reflect with pride, as I have done, on the glorious memories of our beloved Pacific Coast League and your favorite team and players within the league, it will have been worth the effort.

For present-day PCL fans, players and baseball buffs in general, who have an interest in past happenings concerning the game's foremost minor league circuit, I sincerely believe this book will be of interest to you. I know it will to those personally involved in days gone by.

*Ken Stadler*
*Santa Monica, 1984*

# INTRODUCTION

As a baseball fan, I consider myself to have been one of the luckiest persons in the world. Why? Because I grew up in Pacific Coast League territory. If you feel sorry for me for not having been raised in a major league city, don't be. I was fortunate because the Pacific Coast League could not be topped when it came to minor league baseball. Further, I was blessed because being a PCL fan for twenty years meant that I saw baseball's greatest players—past, present and future. I don't think it's overstating the case to say that of all the minor leagues, none could challenge the Pacific Coast League where individual records are involved, be they seasonal or lifetime.

Great baseball players have literally played a career in the PCL. Foremost among this type of player were pitcher Herm Pillette and outfielder Arnold "Jigger" Statz. Together, these men piled up forty-one years of play in the League. Statz set records that will never be topped. Many former greats furthered their careers here, after years of fruitful major league service. Still many other excellent ballplayers moved up to the majors from this League. This particular mode of operation was a common procedure during the 20-year span of which I write. It brought the League to the very brink of major league status. So certain were PCL officials that this would happen, the League declared Open Classification in 1952, a move intended to pave the way for the PCL to join the major leagues.

So strong were many Coast League teams that I do not hesitate to say they could have easily disposed of several clubs on the major league scene today.

Unbelievable attendance records were also attained, particularly during those years immediately following World War II.

Yes, we had a lot going for us, baseball-wise, on the West Coast. I'm so glad I availed myself of it, especially since I'm convinced that minor league baseball will never achieve such heights again. Regrettably, two-thirds of the success formula has been removed. Gone are the outstanding minor league "career-players." And gone are the players who could still greatly contribute to the game at the close of their playing days in the major leagues (most simply retire). This leaves only the players on their way up. The point is that this triangular structure of the Coast League meant that I saw and enjoyed great baseball, albeit the minor leagues. And I have only the happiest of memories, some of which I want to share with you. They are offered for your enjoyment and reading pleasure. The author has no intention or desire that you the readers consider him by any means an authority on the PCL. I have simply done what hundreds of others could have accomplished as well or better than I, had they chosen to do so. We'll discuss a number of subjects involving situations, people, places, things, trivia, and yes, some of those ever-present statistics. Really, we are just going to have a little chat. Nothing I say will be too long or drawn out.

So, whether you are young or old, relax and enjoy one man's memories about the good old Pacific Coast League days.

# Gilmore Field
## AND THE
# Hollywood Stars

# PACIFIC COAST LEAGUE REALIGNS

THE YEAR 1958 brought much excitement to the cities of Los Angeles and San Francisco. Major league baseball had arrived on the West Coast. The Brooklyn Dodgers moved to Los Angeles, while the New York Giants began play in historic Seals' Stadium in San Francisco. It was inevitable that these two cities would achieve major league status, and although I was happy to see this happen, there was a feeling of sadness that settled over me. It closed 20 years of following the PCL. It likewise marked the end of 55 years of continuous play in the League for both Los Angeles and San Francisco. Oakland came close, having been in the PCL 53 consecutive years (1903–1955). The Oakland franchise was shifted to Vancouver, B.C., where the new Vancouver Mounties began PCL play in 1956. The Oakland move was perhaps the first inkling that a major league team was coming to the Bay Area. One year later, in 1957, the Brooklyn Dodgers purchased the minor league rights to the Angels from the parent Chicago Cubs, which clearly indicated that Walter O'Malley would attempt to bring the Dodgers to Los Angeles, which he successfully did in 1958.

Yes, the coming of the Dodgers to Los Angeles and the arrival of the Giants in San Francisco indeed meant realignment. Los Angeles moved to Spokane, Washington, while Hollywood shifted to Salt Lake City, Utah. San Francisco transferred to Phoenix, Arizona, and became the number one farm team of the Giants. Phoenix is still a Triple-A affiliate of San Francisco.

Well, let's back up from that year of 1958, which saw the restructuring of the PCL, and reminisce a bit as we relive One Man's Memories covering the years of 1938 to 1957.

# GILMORE FIELD AND THE HOLLYWOOD STARS

Beginning at the corner of Beverly Boulevard and Fairfax Avenue, and extending several blocks eastward, was located Los

Angeles' most prestigious sports complex. There was old Gilmore Stadium, once the home of the Los Angeles Dons of the old All-America Football Conference, as well as several other professional football teams. Loyola University of Los Angeles also played their home games here, as did several high schools. There was the beautiful Pan Pacific Auditorium. Here is where all the ice shows were staged. College basketball and minor league ice hockey aided in keeping this arena busy the year around.

Between Gilmore Stadium and the Pan Pacific stood Gilmore Field, the home of the Hollywood Stars. It was a wooden structure with a covered grandstand. Open bleacher sections extended from the end of the grandstand to both the left and right field fences. It had the usual ticket booths, bunched together outside the main entrance, and even though baseball was played here for 19 years it gave every evidence of being a temporary structure. Knowing that a handle such as "beautiful" could never be hung on it, zealous PR men and all of us Star fans simply knew it as "friendly Gilmore Field."

It was, to me, the perfect description. My life as a boy and young man would never have been as happy or my interest in baseball fully realized were it not for this grand old park. It is a fact that I saw many games here as a boy, but as a high-schooler and young man I saw even more contests, rarely missing a series. Some buddy and I were there every time the team was home. When I was still too young to drive, we could reach the park by taking only two buses. I remember when attending day games we'd always arrive around 10 a.m. This meant we would have to kill a couple of hours before the gates opened. This we generally did by hanging around the nearby Farmer's Market. Whatever we did, I couldn't wait for the time to come that would find us in the ball yard. Of course, I just knew the Stars were going to win when I was there. I was crushed when this didn't always happen. The only time I could tolerate defeat was when my favorite player Joe Brovia beat us with his good bat. When you are truly a fan, there is no in-between feeling. When you win, it's heaven; when you lose, you're desolate. That after-the-game hamburger always tasted better when we had just humbled the opposition. If you've never had such feelings after a game, it's my conclusion that you are a spectator, not A FAN.

After purchasing a ticket and rushing through the turnstile, I generally bought a program before heading into the park. If it was early, and it most often was, I would make a right turn and go about 30 feet under the grandstand. There on the wall would be the Stars' starting lineup. Management prepared a large drawing of the playing field. Over each position was a picture of each Hollywood player who would play that day or night. They always kept it up to date; I never remember its being wrong. This innovation was not a part of management policy throughout Gilmore Field's 19-year history. I remember it in the mid-1940s. I like to think this was peculiar to Gilmore Field, though maybe you've seen it done somewhere else.

But before we enter the ballpark itself, allow me to tell you how I first became acquainted with the Hollywood Stars. The year was 1938. As a very young boy, I remember turning the dial on my old but rather large Zenith table model radio early one evening. Suddenly, I came across a Stars game in progress. I heard for the first time such names as Uhalt, Brenzel and Hoover. It was the beginning of an association which would last for 20 years.

As a statistical point, it should be noted that Hollywood first came into the League in 1926 and remained a part of it until the end of the 1935 season. Strangely enough, during that ten-year period they never played a game within the community of Hollywood, even though the team bore its name. After a two-year absence, they returned and remained the Hollywood Stars from 1938 to 1957. During their first year back in the League, Stars' home games were played at Wrigley Field. Wayne Osborne pitched the '38 opener and it was the only time in his fourteen-year career that he got a starting assignment in an initial league game. Gilmore Field opened its gates in 1939.

Even though Gilmore Field did indeed open in 1939, it was not in time for the Stars to play their first home stand there. Where do you think they played—Wrigley Field? No, they played next door at Gilmore Stadium, of all places. The team opened on the road and when they returned from up north, Gilmore Field was not quite ready so they settled for a brief period of time on the infield of a stadium which, at that time, was used primarily for midget auto racing.

Having been in Gilmore Stadium many times in later years, and recalling its oval shape, I reasoned that, depending on the layout, either the left or right field fence would have to be quite short, i.e., L.A. Coliseum–Dodger Baseball. Well, thanks to the information supplied by former Hollywood pitcher Wayne Osborne, I can tell you that the short fence was in right field, and it was *extremely* short, being no more than 200 feet from home plate, but most likely even shorter than that. A ground rule was put into effect which stated that a ball hit into the right field bleachers had to carry so many rows before it could be called a home run. Anything short of the determined distance was a double. Wayne pitched the first game in this makeshift baseball park which had to be equal to or better than the thrill he received one year earlier when he pitched the initial game of the Stars' 1938 season. Wayne lost the '39 home opener 340–1 on a homer by Seattle outfielder Art Hunt. Being a sore loser I'll bet it was one of those cheap right-field homers. Osborne, displaying a delightful sense of humor, once related that an even bigger thrill came in 1942 when Hollywood traded him to Portland. The very next week after the trade the Stars and Beavers met in a series and Wayne beat Hollywood twice in that week. He jokingly admits that he must be a revengeful sort of person.

That old Zenith was to be my only contact with the Stars until the early 1940's, when I attended my first game at Gilinore Field.

# THE ANNOUNCERS

Mike Frankovich was the first radio announcer I remember. I can still hear those old Wheaties commercials:

*"Have you tried Wheaties, the best breakfast food in the land;*
*Have you tried Wheaties, they're whole wheat with all of the bran."*

Later, Fred Haney and Woody Hattic became Hollywood announcers. They always signed off each game by saying "This is Fred Haney and Woody Hattic rounding third and heading for home." Haney was unusual, in that he would recapitulate at the close of each half inning, stating everything that happened. It was very simple to do this in a one-two-three inning, but believe me, it got complicated when a team would score a bunch of runs by way of hits, errors and walks. He never failed to do this phase of his broadcast accurately. I have not heard an announcer before or since do this, and I liked it. Hattic, incidentally, would double as the public address announcer. Later, his sole job was that of PA man.

Then there was old Charlie Tees, who for a period of years recreated road games. Even for a fan, these were not too interesting.

Later, it was the late Mark Scott and Dick Schadt who called the Star's games. These two stole the idea from the San Diego broadcasters of ringing a bell to signify how many runs the Stars scored. This bell ringing took place at the conclusion of their time at bat. The bell was never transported for use away from home. The Los Angeles broadcasters never bothered with this idea, except as an adaptation when Hollywood invaded Wrigley Field for a series. Angel television announcer Bill Brundage would go over to USC and borrow their air horn, which used to be popular at college games. Whenever the Angels scored, that thing would sound off. It made the little Hollywood chime sound like the tinkle of the tiny bell in your parakeet's cage. I admit, it was a great idea and an integral part of the Hollywood–Los Angeles rivalry.

By the way, when television entered the scene, Tom Harmon, Fred Hessler and Bill Welsh called the play for the Stars' games.*

## GET READY TO ENTER THE GRANDSTAND

We are now going to enter the grandstand, and not only see a good baseball game, but look at many fascinating people, happenings, and things of interest as they come to mind concerning Gilmore Field and the Hollywood Stars.

The grandstand and box seats were accessible from the turnstiles by several short stairways containing no more than 10 or 15 steps. Upon arriving at the top, I would stop just long enough to see who was taking batting practice and then I'd turn and take my seat, most generally midway up. I always enjoyed the pre-game happenings on the field, and was in awe of super-talented players, regardless of who they played for. For example, when No. 23, Joe Brovia, took batting practice I was literally captivated by this man's bat. No game was really complete without being able to watch batting practice and a sharp infield drill. When I missed these I felt cheated.

---

*The press box at Hollywood was located just beneath the grandstand roof and could only be reached by a narrow catwalk. It was rather small and used exclusively by the news media. Radio and TV announcers and Woody Hattic worked out of the lower grandstand or box seat areas. Messages were relayed to Hattic by attaching them to a cable. Sheer gravity got them to their destination.

Already a number of other memories have come to mind. For instance, I recall the park's public address speakers barking out the batting order of the game which would soon begin. My ears would strain to catch the announcer's voice as I quickened in anticipation.

# PUBLIC ADDRESS ANNOUNCER

There may have been others, but Woody Hattic was the only PA announcer I remember at Hollywood. He was a likeable, outgoing man with a clear, articulate voice so important for his job. I recall him as being a short, somewhat pudgy individual with a receding hairline. He always wore a suit and tie and looked the sharp dresser. I had the privilege of sitting in the box seats next to his booth one night when Portland was in town. Every time Ed Basinski would come to bat I tried to get him to announce Basinski as "the Fiddler," Eddie being an accomplished violinist. Although Hattic was a friendly and jovial man and seemed to enjoy my kibitzing, he played it straight concerning Ed Basinski. He openly engaged my buddy and me in conversation throughout the entire game. I remember thinking how great it was that this important man could be so casually chatting with two young high school students. Believe it or not, that was the only time I ever sat in the box seats at Gilmore Field.

# THE VENDORS

Vendors have always played a big part at sporting events. Many times I have asked myself the question: Are these people here to see a baseball game, or to eat? Of course, I too have bought my share of peanuts and hot dogs, and often went home with mustard on my shirt and pants, making my mother less than happy, since Biz had not yet been invented.

Well, Gilmore Field had an abundance of interesting men busy hawking their wares. My first recollection of a vendor is the man who sold the novelty items. A short, heavyset individual, he appeared just totally burdened down with all that the word "novelty" implies. Even though he goes back to the very early days, I remember his famous line. "What are you gonna take home to little Willie?" He never said anything more, or anything less, than that patented phrase.

Then there was the immaculate hot dog vendor. This man was dressed just like a chef, complete with hat. The heavy apparatus that he carried had a steam compartment for the franks as well as spaces for the buns and condiments. Each dog was made to order and served on a clean piece of waxed paper. To the direct opposite of him, there was a famous beer vendor, a large man and completely dedicated to the task of selling brew. Perspiration literally ran off of him as he hurried up and down the aisles. The thing I remember about this fellow was that he had no line, just good lungs. At short intervals he would blast out, saying only "BEER!!" Granted, the ballpark was small, but be the crowd quiet or loud, large or small, this man could be heard to the far reaches of the bleacher seats—which were located far down each line. I am a teetotaler, but I must admit this guy came close to selling me on several occasions. He was indeed a very interesting merchant, and always sold out before the other dispensers of brew.

The program sellers were perhaps the least vocal of all the vendors, because people's minds were generally made up as to whether or not they wanted a program. Since programs were also available as you entered the park, little or no persuasive tactics were used inside the stadium. Hollywood, incidentally, had a very impressive multi-page program, complete with player sketches, the usual advertisers, team rosters, and a score sheet. By contrast, the Angels sold only an elongated, stiff score card.

By the way, the late Danny Goodman was the concessionaire at Hollywood in the 1950s. As many of you know, he held that position for the Los Angeles Dodgers. If Hollywood had an edge in the area of concessions, it could largely be attributed to this man.

Many vendors made a career by working the different sports events. I'd see them at work in several places and at different times of the year. No youths, such as we see today, ever worked as vendors, ticket sellers or ticket takers at Gilmore Field, to my recollection.

### TUMMY vs. BALL GAME

*I went out to the ballpark for to see my favorites play.*
*Others were there also, who cared not about the fray.*
*At least it seemed that way to me, for in a little while*
*Up jumps two kids in front of me. They're heading for the aisle.*

*They spot the ice cream vendor and hot dog man on his way.*
*The problem is, when they stood up I missed a double play.*
*In the fifth a mighty Libke blast brought us from behind.*
*But I failed to see that shot—four girls had peanuts firm in mind.*

*We got into the ninth frame with the score tied one to one;*
*Three thirsty men passed by me as Gladd scored the winning run.*
*Well, that's part of baseball. I saw no need to be up tight.*
*In spite of all that happened...I'll be back tomorrow night.*

KS

# THE ADVERTISERS

Gilmore Field had the usual large advertisements on the outfield walls which were so common in minor league, and even earlier major league parks. Restaurants, clothiers and car dealerships were some of the businesses that bought space at Hollywood. Of course, there was always a large ad for Mobil Service stations, and before that, the Gilmore Oil Company always had on display a large ad. Some of you know Mobil Oil purchased the Gilmore Company and merged their stations into Mobil.

I remember the large Gilmore family home that was located right on the property between Gilmore Stadium and Gilmore Field. It resembled a Spanish hacienda, with cactus and pottery in evidence everywhere and the whole estate protected by a large wall completely enclosing it.

Getting back to advertisers, I remember one company (which shall remain nameless) who came up with a different advertising twist. They mounted their ad above the outfield walls. One sign was in left field and the other in right field; both were circular in design and somewhere between three and four feet in diameter. Of course, any ball that hit them was a home run. The company gave $100 to any player who hit either sign. Paul Pettit told me that he once hit the sign in right field and almost had to go in on bended knee to get his money. He felt the company was reluctant to hand over the cash since they felt him to be wealthy because of his bonus contract.

# THE SCOREBOARD

In dead center field was located a rather modest scoreboard. It was lit by seven or eight conventional but large light bulbs protected by a metal shield which, of course, faced the field of play. The runs were hand-mounted and painted red with a white background when the inning was still in progress, and black when the inning was completed. The ball and strike count showed in green and red lights, green for the balls and red for strikes. Scores of other PCL games also showed here. Major league scores were only given by the public address announcer. This scoreboard would rank with the modest of the modest, and in no way could be compared with the one at Wrigley Field, which was remarkably modern for that time.

## GLOVES IN THE OUTFIELD

How many of you can remember when it was common for outfielders to leave their gloves in the outfield while their team was at bat? Believe me, it was a regular procedure at Gilmore Field for years. They were always left at or near the cut of the outfield grass. In retrospect, I can't imagine how this practice ever got started or was allowed to remain for so long. I can't say I personally ever saw a player step on one, nor can I say that I ever saw a ball deflect off of one. I would have to believe that there was a ground rule involving balls that bounced off these gloves. As for the injury risk, the best insurance is to remove the problem. This, of course, they eventually did. I'm beginning to feel old when I reminisce about this point-in-time.

## THE BACKSTOP SCREEN, SHORT PANTS AND BATTING HELMETS

Of note concerning Gilmore Field was its large backstop screen. Not only did it protect the fans seated directly behind home plate, but it extended all the way to the dugouts down each line. Although it made getting a souvenir baseball more difficult, I personally liked the added protection. Angel fans were known to say that the ball club was cheap, hence the large screen. I do remember during World War II that no one was allowed to keep a baseball that did make it into the stands. The owners of the Stars placed several large barrels in strategic locations throughout the park where ushers deposited them. Each barrel was painted red, white and blue. Every ball that they retrieved would be distributed to various military camps for use by the GI's. Few fans made any fuss about surrendering baseballs under these conditions.

In all of my years of viewing games at Hollywood I never came close to catching a baseball. Reserve San Diego outfielder Dick Greco once tossed my buddy a used ball during pregame warmups in 1948 as we were leaning over the railing, and that's the closest I've come.

Speaking of the military, I did miss two years of PCL baseball because of time spent in Uncle Sam's club. The years were 1951 and 1952, during which time I kept up with PCL baseball by way of local, newspapers. I believe that during this time Hollywood came out with its short pants. They resembled Bermuda shorts and were only worn during the warm summer months. From the pictures I've seen of them, they revealed many a bony knee and leg, often exposing what most folks had heretofore thought to be a fine athletic physique. I believe also that at this time the Pittsburgh Pirates began experimenting with batting helmets. They soon became mandatory, and that included their Hollywood Farm team. We all know the result of that experiment.

I remember when outfielder Frankie Hawkins was beaned years earlier. It was touch and go for a while but he did recover. And I was in the ballpark the day they carried Hollywood catcher "Moose" Krause off the field on a stretcher. Krause was particularly vulnerable to being hit by a ball riding in on him, since he had a large stride into the pitch.

## SHORTEST HOME RUN

In my time I've seen many home runs hit at Gilmore Field. I remember seeing my favorite Hollywod player, Paul Pettit, hit two home runs on opening day of the 1956 season. He narrowly missed a third which went foul at the last second. Hollywood outfielder Bill Causion cleared the center field wall in the mid-1950s, making him one of a select group ever to accomplish that feat. Without doubt, the late slugging Hollywood outfielder Frank Kelleher was the man I personally saw hit more home runs at Gilmore Field than any other player. He consistently hit his homers on a line, which meant they went out of the ballpark in a hurry. You might say they were in direct contrast with the "Ruthian clouts" which sailed high and long off the bat of the immortal Babe.

I don't know if what I'm about to tell you holds the record as the shortest home run ever hit at Gilmore Field, but I recall it that way. Hollywood, rather than using chalk to identify the outfield foul lines, buried pieces of wood running end-to-end from the cut of the outfield grass all the way to the left and right field fences. The wood was painted white and no one knew where the chalk on the infield left off and the painted wood began. I sure was unaware of it until one night Lee Walls hit an opposite field hump-back liner that landed just on the corner of the wood and caromed back into fair ground. The fielder, never thinking the ball would react in such a manner, overran it. This, coupled with some poor handling by various infielders, gave Walls an inside-the-park homer. It left me literally fatigued after having rooted him around the bases. This incident was in all respects a hilarious situation which kept many of us fans limp from laughter for quite some time afterwards. The whole scene would have fit in well with some of those baseball bloopers the TV networks so often put together for us nowadays.

# OPENING DAY CEREMONIES

Quite frankly, I was never one to care about opening day festivities or other first ball ceremonies that took place during the course of a season. If Hollywood management desired to have Mrs. Birdie Feathers throw out the first ball in honor of her intense interest in the preservation of the Semi-Bald North American Eagle, it was all right with me. However, since I was and still am ready for spring training the next day after the final out which brought to a close the baseball season, I don't like anything that delays the start of the old ball game. I realize these ceremonies are in order, but believe me, at the minor league level very few people really care.

I have attended a lot of opening day games (few were ever scheduled at night) at Hollywood. The first ball honor on several occasions went to the late Toastmaster General Georgie Jessel. I don't know whether he was purposely scheduled so often, or was a designated substitute for, let's say, Marilyn Monroe, who once declined the offer. Whatever the case, I remember old Georgie doing the honors more than once. One year a motorcade was organized. Hollywood players rode in convertibles and were in uniform. The cars, of course, went up famous Hollywood and Sunset Boulevards before working their way back to Gilmore Field. If memory serves me right, Jessel participated in this. Jessel was known for his patriotism and love of young women, though probably not in that order. But for some reason, he always came alone to these opening day ceremonies.

Since we are spending so much time on Georgie Jessel, I remember a sketch Bob Hope did years ago, where an aspiring actress asked him, "What advice would you give to young actresses?" Hope's facetious answer was, "Stay away from Georgie Jessel."

Well, regardless of how I felt about these ceremonies, it was opening day and I cared a lot about that. The opening day game of 1956 was the one I remember enjoying the most.

# THE GAMBLERS

Characteristic of Gilmore Field, as well as your own favorite park, were the ever-present gamblers who regularly placed their bets at each game. It took me a few years to pick them out, but after having done so I thoroughly enjoyed observing their behavior. I so well remember how they would gather together outside the stadium and talk it over before going in. On several occasions I made it a point to move in close enough to listen to their chatter. They were dead serious and acted like handicappers at the old race track. As you might suspect, these men were the somewhat alcoholic, older citizens of that day and their clothes gave evidence of too much use and lack of care. Not only did their clothes give evidence of too much use, but their breath and actions gave evidence of too much nipping. The more patronage they gave my favorite beer vendor or any of the other dispensers of suds, the more interesting the situation became among these boys (they always sat together). Especially was this true when the lead would change from one team to the other. I recall a few shoving matches, but mostly words only were exchanged. All of this had to add up to the fact that the losers did not subtract too much money from their savings. These fellows were most interesting, to say the least. Some of their faces are vividly implanted in my mind's eye.


### THE GAMBLING FAN

*A vital part of baseball was a certain threadbare clan.*
*They hung around together and were called the Gambling Fan.*
*They always talked it over just outside the ballyard gate.*
*Their bets were placed in earnest as to the ballgame's fate.*

*Some felt they'd be a winner when old Red Munger took the hill.*
*But they knew they were a loser when Lucky Lohrke pitched*
        *the pill.*
*One chanced and raised the ante, sensing a booming Kelleher clout.*
*But he wished he'd kept his mouth shut when Big Frank so*
        *quick struck out.*

*There were often disagreements, each one thinking he was right.*
*There'd be some loud words spoken, now and then a short-lived*
        *fight.*
*One thing they had in common—the need to down some brew.*
*They satisfied the longing, and hoisted not a few.*
*A cloud of smoke engulfed them as to the smoking lamp they'd*
        *yield.*
*It was the proof of puffin' on Lucky Strike or Chesterfield.*

*When the last out was recorded, the victors sought their*
        *proper due.*
*It never really came to more than just a buck or two.*

                                                        *KS*

# HORSEHIDE HASH

Under this seemingly unpalatable title, I'd like to briefly throw a few subjects of lesser import into the pot. I hope they won't be too hard to digest.

*MUSIC*—Nowadays, music at baseball games is an everyday occurrence, especially on the major league scene. Not only do we have melodious organ strains before the games and between innings, but we have it during the game. For instance, if "Slugging Sidney" happens to be from Terre Haute, we can look forward to a few bars of *Back Home Again in Indiana* as he approaches the plate. Or, if "Hard-Hitting Harry" drives in a couple of runs, we've come to expect the organist to play a measure or two of *More* as "Mad Dog Marvin" takes his place in the batter's box. Somehow we survived without this in the PCL. Music was limited to holiday and Sunday games, where I remember some classy Dixieland groups performing at Gilmore Field. They were really good. I can still hear the fine rendition of *South Rampart Street Parade*. These groups added a lot and were always in good taste. Incidentally, my first experience with organ music was in the PCL. It was in 1958 at San Diego's new Westgate Park.

*HOME RUN CONTESTS*—This form of pregame entertainment was the most widely used, and generally involved three or four players from the home and visiting teams. It seemed to me that more often than not the big sluggers had difficulty in these contests. Managers were pretty wise in their selections. By that I mean, in addition to the big boys, they would often throw in a hitter who, during the heat of battle, couldn't hit the breaking ball or off-speed pitch, but could rip the fast ball out of the park. Since the fast ball was all they got during these contests, they quite often came out on top.

*EGG-THROWING CONTESTS*—No, this was not a contest to see who could most often hit the home plate umpire from fifty feet away. It involved sets of two; a player from each team would form a pair. Fresh eggs were brought out. The players would start facing each other at close range, throwing the eggs underhanded. After each catch, both players would step back one foot. This continued until the eggs shattered in someone's hand. The last team to survive claimed a victory. Granted, this type of thing was simple, but I believe the players and fans alike enjoyed it.

*LUCKY NUMBER GIVEAWAYS*—On quite a regular basis, drawings were held at Gilmore Field. These lucky numbers appeared on certain pages of the souvenir program. I remember free dinners were often awarded from restaurants on La Cienega's Restaurant Row.

*FAN BATTING NIGHT*—Fan involvement in pregame activities virtually never happened. I do remember an occasion at Gilmore Field when fans were given three swings each. This was run off in rapid order to accommodate as many as possible. To my knowledge no prizes were awarded for distance hitting. The promotion was merely used to bring fans into the ballpark.*

# HOLLYWOOD–LOS ANGELES RIVALRY

Anticipating that you might be expecting something from me concerning a long-lasting, bitter rivalry between these two Los An- geles area teams, I do want to touch on that subject. In all candor, I personally cannot give you numerous bits of information that you might expect would be forthcoming. I will not, however, sidestep this subject or the one or two others where you might suspect many exciting incidents would flood my memory, but simply do not.

There was indeed a rivalry of sorts on the field and in the communications media. The late Angel radio broadcaster Bob Kelly did his best to stir up the fans by being less than kind to Hollywood personnel. He effectively did this from behind the mike during his play-by-play. He further kept the pot boiling by firing many a verbal shot at the Stars through his nightly radio sports show that aired for many years. I do admit he penetrated my tender skin more than once, and I surely felt the pain from his

---

*Attendance was up when some of Hollywood's brightest starlets would take part in a pre-PCL baseball game. This "game" seemed to make the regularly scheduled contest anticlimactic.

attack. Being rather abrasive and super Angel-minded typified Bob Kelly to a tee.

Of course, he accomplished what he set out to do: namely pit Angel fans against Star rooters. As a result, attendance was always up when these two teams got together. I've seen overflow crowds extending into the outfield for their games at Hollywood. Many a time I took the old Vermont streetcar to the ballpark at 42nd and Avalon for an Angel–Star series, thereby making my contribution to the Wrigley Chewing Gum fortune.

Insofar as any retort from Hollywood announcers was concerned Mark Scott would often get in some digs. Be assured, however, that he was in no way, shape or form in Bob Kelly's league when it came to effective needling.

As was the case with Bob Kelly, it is my belief that no love was lost between Angel television announcer Bill Brundage and anyone or anything connected with the Hollywood Stars. Brundage, however, got his licks in by seeking to upstage any and all Star gimmickry, thereby agitating Hollywood in a different way.

Before the advent of Bob Kelly, and later Brundage, there was really nothing more than a mutual admiration society in the communications media as regards both teams' announcers. In looking back, I really liked what Kelly achieved. It was good for the intra-city rivalry. At the same time, I do remember not liking him very much, which clearly indicates how thoroughly he got to me.

Before a brief statement concerning the players themselves, I want to say, insofar as newspaper reporting involving the two teams was concerned, especially when they played each other, we received excellent, frank and efficient coverage. Representing the sports departments of Los Angeles' newspapers were such men as Ned Cronin, Braven Dyer, Bob Hunter, Al Santoro and Al Wolf. These men deserved the label *super writers*. If, however, their intent was to create a rivalry fraught with tension and unhappiness between the fans and players, it never fully registered with me.

As for the players themselves, I want to tell you of one incident that left one former Angel third baseman very angry and bitter with the Hollywood players and the Star organization. Murray Franklin played third base for Hollywood in 1950 and 1951, later played part of the 1953 season with the Angels after starting the campaign with San Diego. During a game in '53 Franklin figured in two bang-bang plays at third base during an Angel–Stars game at Gilmore Field.

Both incidents involved the same base runner, Ted Beard. The fact that the same runner would have occasion to slide into third base twice in the same game is somewhat unusual, but it happened that afternoon. Beard, who was a short but scrappy player, roughed up Franklin pretty good on his first slide, but nothing came of it. I recall no ill feelings being visible from the stands, if indeed there were any. Beard's second shot at Franklin, though, resulted in a good slugfest which saw the usual bench-clearing and commotion that follows. Beard came in with both feet high, spiking Franklin — and he totally lost his cool.

To my knowledge, Murray never got over that incident. He was most vocal in his dislike for Ted Beard and the entire Hollywood organization. I remember in subsequent years when Hollywood and Los Angeles old-timers games were played, he never appeared in a Hollywood uniform. He did play in several games involving former Angels.

I'm glad I don't recall too many incidents such as I witnessed between Beard and Franklin. This one was enough and admittedly is distasteful for me to pass on. What I do like to remember as a constant part of the rivalry stems from how it pertained to the fans. I recall cheers, jeers and undignified use of the King's English. The purchase of a ticket did not bring with it the censure of the tongue. Aside from abusive language, I'm glad it didn't. This was a big part of Hollywood–Los Angeles baseball![*]

In attempting to figure out why this rivalry and the other natural rivalries were only occasionally intense, I could only blame it on the constant changing of uniforms within the League of ever so many players. This uniform-switching, of course, involved quite a few players who played for both Hollywood

---

[*]Nineteen fifty-three was a big year for Ted Beard. He hit .286, hit safely in twelve consecutive times at bat, and hit four consecutive home runs in one game.

and Los Angeles. Many of these players were simply with their respective teams too short a time to become attached or totally loyal to just one team. Under the heading *"Longevity List"* (which appears later), aside from Jigger Statz and a few others, every man played for at least two or more teams in the PCL. *Many players played many years in the Coast League, but to pin any player down to one, two or three teams for any extended period of time was virtually impossible.*

Yes, there was a rivalry that existed between these two Los Angeles area teams. I, however, am satisfied to accept the fact that, in the main, Star and Angel players viewed their local competition pretty much the same as they did any other PCL team. *This is not to say they didn't give it their all.* These are my sincere feelings, right or wrong.

## PLAYERS WHO PLAYED ON BOTH TEAMS

The following is my unofficial list of players who wore both uniforms:

| | | |
|---|---|---|
| Lee Anthony | Gene Handley | Tom Saffell |
| Jim Baxes | Red Lynn | Jack Salveson |
| Fern Bell | Eddie Malone | Eddie Sauer |
| Tod Davis | Butch Moran | Bill Schuster |
| Murray Franklin | Bob Muncrief | Lou Stringer |
| George Freese | Willie Ramsdell | Bill Sweeney |
| Gordon Goldsberry | John Rothrock | |

I listed Gene Handley as having been with both teams, although he really was not. Los Angeles named Handley as manager for the 1958 season. The coming of the Dodgers to Los Angeles for the 1958 campaign took care of that. To my knowledge, he did not remain as manager when the Angels moved to Spokane. Gene was a manager that was not.

# THE GAME IS STILL THE THING

Needless to say, the games themselves are the reason you and I really go to the stadium. Since it would be impossible for me to select one most important or exciting game, just let me say that to me, *every* game I attended at Gilmore Field was exciting. *This I really mean.* I was always happy to be there, and never went under coercion from anyone. Many players of varying capabilities, styles and personalities often flash through my mind whenever I reflect on the hundreds I've seen in a Hollywood uniform. Additionally, there are several non-playing personalities who clearly remain in my mind.

I believe I can best sum up this section on Gilmore Field and the Hollywood Stars by discussing favorite Hollywood player personnel, favorite team leaders, and two favorite team employees.

# FIRST PLAYER REMEMBERED

BERNARD "FRENCHY" UHALT was the first player that I remember, and he was an early favorite of mine. He hit .322 in 1938 and played in 166 games. He had a minor league lifetime batting average of .300. He had a total of 3,120 hits and 899 RBI's in 20 years of minor league play. Uhalt played five years with Hollywood before being traded to San Francisco after the 1942 season. He finished his Coast League career in 1948 with Oakland, which ironically was the team he began Coast League play with in 1928. The former Bakersfield all-around athlete was a very durable and consistent professional baseball player. I listed him as an outfielder on my all-time Hollywood team.

Uhalt always hit well in day games and very much disliked night baseball because of the poor lighting in many parks. Be that as it may, this man ranks very high among those I was fortunate enough to see play in the PCL. Many players would have been happy to have done as well.

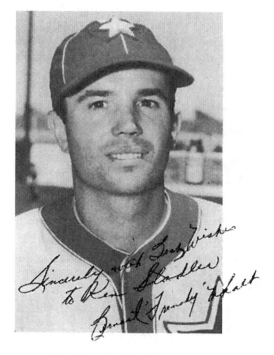

## TWO FORMER
## MAJOR LEAGUE GREATS

The League, in addition to being known for its own outstanding players, was also blessed by the appearance of numerous major league greats who closed their careers in the PCL. I wish to comment on only two of these players, ones particularly special to me in the early years. Both played with Hollywood.

**FLOYD "BABE" HERMAN** was one of the all-time great Brooklyn Dodger hitters. He was the first super hitter from the majors I remember as having played in the Coast League. How well I recall how he could still hit the ball out of the park at a late stage in his career. I've seen him do it in person and listened on the radio as he did it. I remember him primarily as a pinch hitter, having little recollection of seeing him play in the outfield or first base, even though he spent at least six seasons with Hollywood. Some might say this was for the best. since Herman was not known for his work with the glove. The story of his being hit on the head while attempting to catch a baseball was largely the reason why he was ridiculed for his play in the field. You should know, however, that Herman emphatically denies having been hit by a fly ball, and that my PCL records do not show him to be all that bad with the glove.

Many wacky stories were attributed to the Babe, and I confess that I had two tales on him in my manuscript that I fully intended to publish. Although it was painfully embarrassing I am glad I came to grips with the fact that I had wrongfully joined the long list of chroniclers who were *forever* dwelling on some of the silly things that Herman was purported to have done and said, rather than putting the emphasis where it belongs, mainly on his tremendous success as a hitter (his fielding deserved more favorable ink also).

Well, how did Babe Herman do at Hollywood? In the six seasons he played for the Stars, he never hit under .300. Here are his consecutive batting averages from 1939 through 1944: .317, .307, .346, .322, .354 and .346. How many of you know that in 1941 the so-called poor fielder had a fielding percentage of .994 as a first baseman? Les Scarsella was the acknowledged leader, .993, since he played in 169 games to Herman's 66. The Babe hit 42 PCL homers and several times I recall his homering in crucial pinch hitting appearances which resulted in Hollywood victories. He had 301 RBI's as a member of the Hollywood Stars, which he accomplished while playing primarily on a limited basis.

With regard to all the stories written about him, I am absolutely certain in my own mind that if they were true, exaggerated or totally false, I would have thought no less of this man. As a boy I idolized him. If he had had more at bats, I would have named him on my all-time Hollywood team.

I am glad that I now can be counted among what I feel is an ever-increasing number of writers who are bringing to the fore the great talents of Babe Herman, and disdaining that which might elicit a laugh at the expense of truth.

**CHARLIE ROOT** is indeed worthy of comment. I frankly don't have any statistical data on him. I do know he was a successful major league pitcher. The point I wish to make is that he was the Chicago Cub pitcher who served up the home run ball that Babe Ruth "called" in Wrigley Field in 1932. Charlie was over 40 when I saw him pitch at Gilmore Field as a member of the Hollywood Stars. There was an extra excitement I felt in seeing the man who helped the immortal Babe tack on another homer, which would end at 714. This home run hit by Ruth is perhaps the most talked about home run he ever hit. I realize much controversy has arisen concerning Ruth's "called shot" off the pitching slants of Charlie Root. My buddy Rich Timmis, who became acquainted with coach Jimmy Reese, a teammate of Ruth, told me that Reese is clearly of the opinion that Ruth's gesturing did not indicate he was telling the world he would hit a home run. We have all seen the pictures of Babe pointing toward the outfield and we know he was upset. But, alas. I wonder if we will ever know for sure? One thing for certain did happen—Charlie Root became a player of notoriety on that historic afternoon.

Charlie played three seasons with Hollywood: 1942, 1943 and 1944. He was a playing manager in both 1943 and 1944. He won a total of 29 games while losing 24.

## FAVORITE PLAYER

I did settle on one favorite Hollywood player, although this was not easy for me to do. Strangely enough, it was not because of his playing talents (many others were superior), but because of the character and fiber of the man.

**PAUL PETTIT** is my choice. He began as a pitcher after signing a six-digit bonus contract with the Pittsburgh Pirate organization. When arm trouble plagued him, he refused to give up and turned to the outfield and first base. In my opinion he earned a chance to return to the majors, but it never came. No player I ever knew showed more determination or desire to make good in baseball. I became well acquainted with him, and I know whereof I speak. Only the essential physical tools kept him from achieving his goal. He had the distinction of hitting the last home run ever hit at Gilmore Field, in 1957. He hit .284 that year, with 20 home runs and 102 RBI's. Pettit closed his career in the Coast League in the latter 1950s with the Seattle Rainiers.*

# FAVORITE MANAGER

**BOBBY BRAGAN** was my favorite manager. I met him also. I remember staying in the same hotel with the Stars in Oakland (Leamington) during a series in 1955. Bragan supplied box seat tickets for my friend Lloyd Curtis and me for the entire week. That was a fun week if ever there was one.

It was an adventure just getting to Oakland. Lloyd had a 1949 Ford Fordor that was in need of a ring job. We bought a case of cheap oil and would stop every 40 or 50 miles to add a quart to the crankcase. We were able to save some wear and tear by shutting off the motor on the notorious Grapevine at the end of the Ridge Route. We coasted for several miles before heading into Bakersfield, and we finally made it to the Bay Area with a minimum of difficulty.

After the games each night we went to the restaurant where the players always ate. After that, I went back to my room and wrote to the one who was to be my wife. Each night I told her of my love and assured her that she meant more to me than baseball. She has doubted that once or twice over the last 27 years. I know it had to be love, because while I was busy letter-writing, Lloyd—who was already married—was talking base-ball with the players down in the lobby.

Getting back to Bragan, he was a playing manager (catcher) and second only to Chet Johnson for "characters" I have seen in Pacific Coast Baseball. He once, after getting tossed out of a game, lit a cigar, laid down on home plate, crossed his legs and casually puffed away. The most humorous incident I ever recall

---

*If I were to name a favorite Hollywood player strictly on the basis of his play, it would be **Frank Kelleher**. (See additional information on Kelleher under *Most Adept at Hitting Home Runs* on page 142.)

involving Bragan, though, happened in a Stars–Angels game at Wrigley Field. I don't remember what got Bobby angry, but the game was hopelessly lost as far as Hollywood was concerned. He showed his wrath by beginning a parade of pinch hitters, all for what should have been one batter. One man would come up and take a pitch, then Bragan would lift him for another batter. He, in turn, would then take a pitch. If memory serves me right, the count ran out to 3 and 2 before this incident was closed. Six men batted for what should have been one. Most of the pinch hitters were pitchers. This incident earned Bragan a few days off, compliments of the League President. I felt sorry for the public address announcer. Of course, Angel fans were furious. I thought the whole thing was hilarious; I will never forget it. This could have been one way the Stars got back at that old air horn.

I had occasion to talk with Bobby about his suspension shortly after he was set down. He steadfastly maintained that what he had done was perfectly legal and that he had broken no rules of the game. Of course, he was right. They nailed him because his decorum was not befitting a manager. If you know Bragan, for him to have expressed himself in any manner other than the way he handled this situation would simply not be Bragan. More especially, Bobby was an excellent baseball man, having managed several major league teams before moving up to become president of the Texas League, a position he held for many years.

I could close the subject of Bragan right here, but think it fair to say he was not without his detractors, primarily the press. Their disagreement with him did not stem from anything that would suggest his not being a capable manager. Some rumblings of discontent, however, did arise concerning his alleged over-working of certain pitchers. Two former Hollywood pitchers, Bob Garber and Joe Trimble, were the two players in question. They were both starting pitchers who some felt were thrust into too many relief situations to save close games. Both were hard-throwing, highly touted pitchers in the Pittsburgh organization. Neither succeeded in the majors. The question Bragan mal-contents wanted answered was: Did Bobby burn them out at Hollywood? My answer is no. I unhesitatingly say this, be there or be there not any substance to the allegations. I cannot let this matter or his humorous antics sway me from believing that he was a good handler of men, as well as an excellent baseball tactician.

## FAVORITE COACH

GORDON MALTZBERGER is my choice. He was a former Hollywood pitcher with the famous turn-around style used in recent years by Luis Tiant. Maltzberger was basically a quiet man, as I remember him, and seldom if ever involved himself in any verbal altercations. His demeanor had to be beneficial to all players, and his pitching advice of much value to the staff. He served under managers Bragan and King in the 1950s. I was saddened to hear of his death, which took place on December 11, 1974 in Rialto, California.

## FAVORITE INSPIRATIONAL PLAYER

I really believe that anyone who is accorded the recognition of most inspirational player, whether it be given by an individual or group, is really the most honored of all. **MONTY BASGALL**, former second baseman for Hollywood, is my choice. Although he played very little in the major leagues, he was a good, steady Triple-A infielder who quietly went about his job, just working to perfect it.

I remember an incident which I doubt that Basgall himself recalls. The team was struggling and the manager and coaches called a special practice session, requiring only certain players to attend. I recall the radio announcer mentioning that Monty Basgall showed up for that practice even though he was not one of those designated to be there. Is it any wonder that this man is still a respected, highly regarded big league coach? Baseball could use more men like Monty Basgall.

Incidentally, Basgall is the man who successfully converted Dodger outfielders Bill Russell and Davey Lopes into infielders. This keystone combination was recently broken up by the trade of Lopes to Oakland.

# FAVORITE ANNOUNCER

**FRED HANEY** far and away is my choice. I have previously alluded to his style, but I want to mention the tremendous importance of keeping the radio listener abreast of the action by painting an accurate word picture. I was still young when Haney did the play-by-play, but felt I was in the ballpark during his broadcasts. Of course, his being a baseball man aided him immensely.

I'm not, however, suggesting that all former players and managers make good announcers. Even though we kids were always anxious to get players' autographs, I did have the presence of mind to get Fred's name on a program; this before he became manager at Hollywood. He willingly gave it to me; unfortunately for me, I lost it. Even though Hollywood lost him as an announcer, Star fans were happy to see him get back into managing, where he achieved success both with the Stars and later with the Milwaukee Braves. I was particularly happy for him, since he was earlier unsuccessful with the old St. Louis

Browns. Haney's baseball successes continued later when he was the General Manager of the Los Angeles/California Angels of the American League.

# FAVORITE EXECUTIVE

Hollywood had several front office "big wheels"—men like Victor Ford Collins, Bob Cobb and Oscar Reichow. I don't know just why their memory is so vivid to me, but it is. Which one of these men gets my vote for favorite Hollywood executive, you ask? I must tell you, none of them. My vote goes to one **PAUL JESCHKE**, whose title was Secretary-Office Manager, a position he held from 1953 to 1957. Quite honestly, I know nothing of this man's prowess as a leader in high places. I do know that if he had decided to run for public office he would have gotten my vote. He always wore a sharp suit and tie, and smoked a large cigar. All of us regular fans knew who he was. I don't recall going to a game during that five-year period where he didn't make it a point to circulate throughout the ballpark sometime during the course of a game. I remember him as being rather young, tall, and the possessor of the popular crew-cut hairstyle. This boy was a winner. Even though I've long since lost track of him, I just know he was destined to become the chairman of the board of some large corporation.

* * * * *

Beginning at the corner of Beverly Boulevard and Fairfax Avenue and extending several blocks eastward, no longer stands Los Angeles' most prestigious sports complex. Gilmore Stadium and Gilmore Field have long since given way to progress. In their place stands CBS Television City. True, farther up the boulevard the once beautiful Pan Pacific Auditorium still remains. She is in need of much repair and her entrance is covered with weeds. There has been some talk of restoring the building for the sake of posterity, and I hope it happens. One thing we all can keep, though, is our memories of places and people that have meant so much to us. As for Gilmore Field, I will never forget that old ball yard, or the men who played there and all that went into making it such a vital part of my life. I realize it is something special to have major league baseball in my community. Although this is true, I have not been, nor do I expect to be, as involved again in baseball to the extent that I was with my team from Gilmore Field.

# FITTING CONCLUSION

I believe it to be a fitting conclusion to this section to place here these two pictures of my favorite Hollywood player, Paul Pettit, taken in my favorite stadium, Gilmore Field. The picture at the left, taken in 1957, is particularly special to Pettit. He delivered a pinch single during this time at bat, which propelled him into the starting lineup. He went on to lead the Stars in home runs and RBI's and to have his best year in baseball.

**"Paul Pettit was a dedicated baseball player and is a good friend and caring family man."**
**KS**

1939
HOLLYWOOD BASEBALL CLUB
"STARS"

PHOTO BY NEWS PICTURES, LTD.

**HOLLYWOOD STARS – 1955 SEASON**

Top Row, Left to Right: Bob Garber, Lee Walls, Ben Wade, Red Munger, George O'Donnell, George Vico, Joe Trimble.
Middle Row: Frank Jacobs, trainer; George Freese, Curt Roberts, Dick Smith, Bobby Bragan, mgr.; Bill Hall, Bob Prescott, R.C. Stevens.
Bottom Row: Al Zarilla, Bob Del Greco, Cholly Naranjo, Carlos Bernier, Jack Lohrke, Roger Bowman.

# The
# Pacific Coast
# League

# THE PACIFIC
# COAST LEAGUE

The Pacific Coast League was formed in 1903 and comprised six teams:

| Team | Won | Lost | Pct. |
|------|-----|------|------|
| Los Angeles | 133 | 78 | .630 |
| Sacramento | 105 | 105 | .500 |
| Seattle | 98 | 100 | .495 |
| San Francisco | 107 | 110 | .493 |
| Portland | 95 | 108 | .468 |
| Oakland | 89 | 126 | .414 |

The League has had four different classifications since its inception in 1903:

| | |
|---|---|
| Class A | 1903–1907 |
| Class AA | 1908–1945 |
| Class AAA | 1946–1951 |
| Open Classification | 1952–1957 |

# PACIFIC COAST LEAGUE
# PRESIDENTS 1938–1957

| | |
|---|---|
| William C. Tuttle | 1936–1943 |
| Clarence H. (Pants) Rowland* | 1944–1954 |
| Claire V. Goodwin | 1955 |
| Leslie M. O'Connor | 1956–1959 |

---

*Clarence (Pants) Rowland served as president of the PCL longer than anyone else during my time (11 seasons). He ascended to the presidency after being president of the Los Angeles Angels for the 1942 and 1943 seasons. This man guided the League through the difficult war years and beyond. He did so with honor, and was a skilled and respected leader. I know of nothing written or spoken that ever put this man down.

*THE PACIFIC COAST LEAGUE*

*From boy to man I was a fan of the greatest minor league.*
*I followed play in every way and rarely felt fatigue.*

*Just viewing all the action of any Coast League team*
*Was simply the fulfillment of this man's childhood dream.*

*From Frenchy Uhalt to "Mudcat" Grant and others in between,*
*Some of baseball's greatest players made the Coast League scene.*

*Big Joe Brovia and Earl Rapp were the finest hitters I've seen play.*
*They hit above the average and put their power on display.*

*"The Fiddler" Ed Basinski robbed many a batter of a hit,*
*While Carlos "The Bandit" stole some bases whene'er he thought of it.*

*"Chesty Chet," Bobby Bragan and Emmett Ashford were an*
*   entertaining three;*
*They gave a great performance for no added cost or fee.*

*Yes, the major leagues are here to stay and they're surely doing well,*
*But if I had my druthers, I'd take the old but famous PCL.*

*KS*

# PCL'S GREATEST PLAYER

**ARNOLD "JIGGER" STATZ** was foremost among players who achieved greatness in the PCL. Nothing written about the Pacific Coast League would be complete without mentioning this former great Los Angeles outfielder, and I will be no exception.

Statz played 18 years in the League, all with Los Angeles. He holds at least nine PCL records, which I believe it safe to say will never be broken: they border on the unbelievable. One reason they will never be eclipsed is because of the fact that no player will ever again be allowed to play in the PCL long enough to challenge his standing. Even if they were, I'm convinced that no one could match his accomplishments, even if playing under the same circumstances.

I remember Statz as a player and as a playing manager with the Angels. I recall his unusual habit of cutting the leather out of the palm of his glove so that his hand was exposed. He felt it made the ball easier to catch. Who's to argue with this man?

To further illustrate the fact that he was far and away the Coast League's No. 1 player, I can tell you in his 18 seasons with the Angels he had a lifetime batting average of .315. Three times he had over 500 put-outs in a season. He stole a total of 466 bases. In his 19th season in baseball (he played 8 seasons in the majors), Statz had enough speed and savvy of pitchers to steal 43 bases.

Jigger was known to be full of spirit, a quick learner, a brave competitor, a man of impeccable character and one who possessed sportsman-like character. To have been able to get in on the closing years of his career albeit mostly by way of radio was indeed thrilling to me. Those born too late were deprived of seeing play one of baseball's greatest players.

Statz played until he was 45. It is a fact: Jigger Statz was the greatest player who ever played, or ever will play, in the Pacific Coast League!

---

*Dear Ken,*

*Good luck in your writing endeavor.*

*Sincerely, Jigger Statz*

---

## JIGGER STATZ

*The PCL had one man who filled opponent's eyes with tears.*
*He set a heap of records during eighteen glorious years.*
*No player ever came to bat as many times as he;*
*He led the League in most hits, doubles, triples—but then, you see*
*He led in total bases, put-outs and most runs scored.*

*The harder and rougher the challenge, the higher and longer*
   *he soared*
*Far above any other who played in a PCL game.*
*Yes, Jigger Statz is No. 1 in the Coast League's Hall of Fame.*

KS

## PACIFIC COAST LEAGUE HALL OF FAME
### RECORDED APRIL 8, 1944

ARNOLD STATZ                HERMAN PILLETTE
FRANK DILLON                HARRY A. WILLIAMS
EARL SHEELY                 OSCAR VITT
HAP HOGAN                   JOHN BASSLER
RAYMOND FRENCH              J. CARL EWING
H. WILLIAM LANE             JACK LELIVELT
FRANK SHELLENBACK           OTIS CRANDALL
CHARLES H. GRAHAM           CHARLES BAUM
WALTER McCREDIE             FRANK O'DOUL

**Obtained from Lefty O'Doul's restaurant, San Francisco, California.**

# PCL UMPS EXCELLENT ARBITERS

The number of umpires working professional baseball games has depended upon the classification of the leagues. Since the PCL was in Double-A classification when I became involved, there were only two umpires working each game. When the league achieved Triple-A and Open Classification (1946–1957), a third umpire was added. Strange as it may seem, I don't recall there being any more arguments when two or three umpires were used, as compared to the four that work major league games. I imagine much of the reason for this was due to the excellent quality of PCL umpires. Many of them went on to become top-flight umpires in the major leagues.

I liken the quality of umpiring in the PCL to the quality of players. We had top notch minor league players and likewise the umpiring was tops. I am not going to be so naive as to tell you I remember the majority of umps as a boy; that would not be true. As one's interest and knowledge of the game progresses, he broadens his scope and umpires are remembered for their contributions to the game. At least they were with me. I know it would heighten your interest if I could relate some long, drawn out rhubarb, but I cannot remember any worthy of mention. I saw my share, but of the arguments I remember, the over-whelming number were the fault of the player or manager and involved judgment calls where players and/or managers pursued the matter too long. Where rules are involved, I have no recollection other than a protest which was lodged and upheld in 1954.

We often hear that a good boxing referee is conspicuous by his being most often out of the way, though on top of a situation. Maybe this is what I remember most about PCL umpires. Some umpires I recall are:

| | | |
|---|---|---|
| William Englen | Al Mutart | Art Passarella |
| Gordon Ford | Ed Runge | Mel Steiner |
| A1 Somers | Cecil Carlucci | Emmett Ashford |
| Lon Warneke | Gil Stratton | Chris Pelekoudas |
| Pat Orr | Vince Smith | |

Suffice it to say, this is an impressive list of arbiters. All of these I have just listed worked in the major leagues, with the exception of Gil Stratton.

Of interest is the fact that the late American League umpire, Art Passarella, rather than starting his umpiring career in the PCL, ended it there. After resigning as an American League umpire in 1953, he became umpire-in-chief of the Texas League in 1954. He came to the PCL for the 1956 season. Many will remember Passarella as an actor. In addition to appearing in motion pictures, he was perhaps best known for his role as Sgt. Sekuvolich in the television series *The Streets of Sun Francisco*, starring Karl Malden and Michael Douglas. He came into acting on the advice of former PCL infielder Johnny Beradino (more on Beradino to follow). Beradino kiddingly told him that he'd been acting all his life—as an umpire.

From the list of umpires that follows, take notice of the length of service many of them gave to the PCL before making it to the majors. If you do, you'll see these men were not listed just to take up space. Can you imagine any ump nowadays waiting at least 15 years to make it to the majors, as former great PCL umpire Bill Englen did?

---

NOTE: During my time, PCL umpires used both the inside and outside chest protector. I recall no one taking issue with respect to which method was best. As you know, the American League form of umpiring (outside protector) is being phased out by attrition. The death of this decades-long tradition is, to me, one of the greatest tragedies ever permitted in baseball.

# PCL UMPIRE ROSTER

**Class AA**

1938:  Bert Cole              R. W. Snyder
       W. R. Englen          Sam Crawford
       Henry Fanning         C. G. Falls
       Wally Hood            William Doran

1939:  L. E. Edwards         R. W. Snyder
       W. R. Englen          Jack Powell
       Henry Fanning         C. G. Falls
       Wally Hood            William Doran

1940:  W. R. Englen          Jack Powell
       Henry Fanning         C. G. Falls
       Wally Hood            William Doran
       R. W. Snyder          Phillip Guyon Mazzeo

1941:  W. R. Englen          Jack Powell
       Henry Fanning         William Doran
       Wally Hood            L. E. Edwards
       R. W. Snvder          George Jordan
       Dewey Widner

1942:  W. R. Englen          Jack Powell
       Henry Fanning         William Doran
       Wally Hood            L. E. Edwards
       R. W. Snyder          Dewey Widner

1943:  W. R. Englen          L. E. Edwards
       Wally Hood            Dewey Widner
       Jack Powell           Edwin Borski
       William Doran         F. H. McDonald

1944:  W. R. Englen          Dewey Widner
       Jack Powell           Henry Fanning
       William Doran         Gordon Ford
       L. E. Edwards         Ray Snyder

1945:  W. R. Englen          Gordon Ford
       Jack Powell           Robert Kober
       William Doran         Lee Dempsey
       L. E. Edwards         C. G. Falls

## Class AAA

1946:    W. R. Englen          Al Fioresi
Jack Powell           M. Heard
William Doran       John Sears
L. E. Edwards       Al Sommers
Gordon Ford         Lon Warneke
Robert Kober

1947:    W. R. Englen          Lon Warneke
Jack Powell           Pat Orr
William Doran       Edwin Borski
Gordon Ford         Al Mutart
Robert Kober        Phillip Guyon Mazzeo
Al Somers           Ira Gordon

1948:    W. R. Englen          Pat Orr
Jack Powell           Al Mutart
William Doran       Ira Gordon
Gordon Ford         Dan Deever
Al Somers           Joe Rue
Lon Warneke        John Sears

1949:    W. R. Englen          Al Mutart
Jack Powell           Ira Gordon
William Doran       Dan Deever
Gordon Ford         Ed Runge
Al Somers           Lou Barbour
Pat Orr               Roman Bentz

1950:    Jack Powell           Al Mutart
W. R. Englen          Ira Gordon
William Doran       Ed Runge
Gordon Ford         Lou Barbour
Al Somers           Roman Bentz
Pat Orr               Ralph Cunningham
Cecil Carlucci       John Young

1951:    Jack Powell           Al Mutart
W. R. Englen          Ed Runge
William Doran       Lou Barbour
Gordon Ford         Roman Bentz
Al Somers           Cecil Carlucci
Pat Orr               John Young

## Open Classification

| 1952: | Jack Powell | Ed Runge |
| --- | --- | --- |
|  | W. R. Englen | Lou Barbour |
|  | William Doran | Roman Bentz |
|  | Gordon Ford | Cecil Carlucci |
|  | Al Somers | John Young |
|  | Pat Orr | William Anske |
|  | Al Mutart | Joe Iocovetti |
|  | Donald Silva |  |
|  |  |  |
| 1953: | Jack Powell | Roman Bentz |
|  | William Doran | Cecil Carlucci |
|  | Gordon Ford | William Anske |
|  | Al Somers | Joe Iocovetti |
|  | Al Mutart | Don Silva |
|  | Ed Runge | Gil Stratton* |
|  |  |  |
| 1954: | Emmett Ashford | Chris Pelekoudas |
|  | Don Flecky | Al Somers |
|  | Gordon Ford | Gil Stratton |
|  | Mike Hanich | Chris Valenti |
|  | Joe Iocovetti | Gerald Van Keuren** |
|  | Al Mutart | Frank Walsh |
|  |  |  |
| 1955: | Emmett Ashford | Chris Pelekoudas |
|  | William Anske | Vince Smith |
|  | Cecil Carlucci | Al Somers |
|  | Don Flecky | Gil Stratton |
|  | Al Mutart | Chris Valenti |
|  | Pat Orr |  |
|  |  |  |
| 1956: | Emmett Ashford | Art Passarella |
|  | Cecil Carlucci | Chris Pelekoudas |
|  | Gordon Ford | Vince Smith |
|  | Bill Kerr | Al Somers |
|  | Al Mutart | Mel Steiner |
|  | Pat Orr | Steve Yuhase |

---

*Gil Stratton has extensive experience as an actor, but it was his great love for baseball that brought him into umpiring. For many years he has given the sports news on at least two Los Angeles television stations. He always began his remarks by saying, "It's time to call 'em as I see 'em."

1957:    Emmett Ashford        Vince Smith
         Cecil Carlucci        Al Somers
         Bill Kerr             Einer Sorensen
         Pat Orr               Mel Steiner
         Chris Pelekoudas      Steve Yuhase

**Gerald Van Keuren was one of several umps who threw Bobby Bragan out of a game. Bragan reacted to Van Keuren's decision by taking off his cap and bowing low at the waist. Van Keuren tried to ignore it, but finally broke into a broad grin.

NOTE: Bragan's humor was spontaneous and was dependent upon the situation in which he found himself. I sincerely believe that none of Bobby's "humor tantrums" were planned.

*THEM UMPS*

*Only two umps worked each ball game back in 1938.*
*One was stationed on the bases, the other 'hind the plate.*
*This was all that was permitted, 'twas Pacific Coast League's way.*
*The reason's very simple: no more than two in Double-A.*

*In '46 the League moved up a notch to the Class of Triple-A,*
*Which meant another ump was found upon the field of play.*
*No more umps were added as 12 years so fast did pass.*
*The League went on in Triple-A and then to Open Class.*

*There was Englen, Gordon Ford, Pat Orr, and even Ed Runge,*
*Emmett Ashford, Mutart, Gil Stratton and Cecil Carlucci.*
*They called 'em as they saw 'em. But fans seldom did agree.*
*One thing we knew for certain:*
                              *Not one of them could see.*

                                                   *KS*

# PACIFIC COAST LEAGUE MANAGERS
# 1938-1957

## HOLLYWOOD

| | | |
|---|---|---|
| 1938 - Wade Killefer | 1946 - Buck Faucett | 1952 - Fred Haney |
| 1939 - Wade Killefer | 1947 - Jimmy Dykes | 1953 - Bobby Bragan |
| 1940 - Bill Sweeney | 1948 - Jimmy Dykes | 1954 - Bobby Bragan |
| 1941 - Bill Sweeney | Lou Stringer | 1955 - Bobby Bragan |
| 1942 - Oscar Vitt | Mule Haas | 1956 - Clay Hopper |
| 1943 - Charlie Root | 1949 - Fred Haney | 1957 - Clyde King |
| 1944 - Charlie Root | 1950 - Fred Haney | |
| 1945 - Buck Faucett | 1951 - Fred Haney | |

## LOS ANGELES

| | | |
|---|---|---|
| 1938 - Truck Hannah | 1946 - Bill Sweeney | 1954 - Bill Sweeney |
| 1939 - Truck Hannah | 1947 - Bill Kelly | 1955 - Bill Sweeney |
| 1940 - Jigger Statz | 1948 - Bill Kelly | Jack Warner |
| 1941 - Jigger Statz | 1949 - Biil Kelly | Bob Sheffing |
| 1942 - Jigger Statz | 1950 - Bill Kelly | 1956 - Bob Sheffing |
| 1943 - Bill Sweeney | 1951 - Stan Hack | 1957 - Clay Bryant |
| 1944 - Bill Sweeney | 1952 - Stan Hack | |
| 1945 - Bill Sweeney | 1953 - Stan Hack | |

## OAKLAND

| | | |
|---|---|---|
| 1938 - E. H. Zwilling | 1944 - Dolph Camilli | 1950 - Charlie Dressen |
| 1939 - John Vergez | 1945 - Dolph Camilli | 1951 - Mel Ott |
| 1940 - John Vergez | 1946 - Casey Stengel | 1952 - Mel Ott |
| 1941 - John Vergez | 1947 - Casey Stengel | 1953 - Augie Galan |
| 1942 - John Vergez | 1948 - Casey Stengel | 1954 - Charlie Dressen |
| 1943 - John Vergez | 1949 - Charlie Dressen | 1955 - Lefty O'Doul |

## PORTLAND

| | | |
|---|---|---|
| 1938 - Bill Sweeney | 1946 - Marvin Owen | 1954 - Clay Hopper |
| 1939 - Bill Sweeney | 1947 - Jim Turner | 1955 - Clay Hopper |
| 1940 - John Frederick | 1948 - Jim Turner | 1956 - Tommy Holmes |
| 1941 - Oscar Vitt | 1949 - Bill Sweeney | Bill Sweeney |
| 1942 - Frank Brazill | 1950 - Bill Sweeney | 1957 - Bill Sweeney |
| 1943 - Marv Shea | 1951 - Bill Sweeney | Frank Carswell |
| 1944 - Marvin Owen | 1952 - Clay Hopper | Bill Posedel |
| 1945 - Marvin Owen | 1953 - Clay Hopper | |

## SACRAMENTO

| | | |
|---|---|---|
| 1938 - Bill Killefer | 1945 - Earl Sheely | 1951 - Joe Gordon |
| 1939 - Benny Borgmann | 1946 - Earl Sheely | 1952 - Joe Gordon |
| 1940 - Benny Borgmann | 1947 - Dick Bartell | 1953 - Gene Desautels |
| 1941 - Pepper Martin | 1948 - Joe Orengo | 1954 - Gene Desautels |
| 1942 - Pepper Martin | 1949 - Del Baker | Tony Freitas |
| 1943 - Ken Penner | 1950 - Ralph Kress | 1955 - Tony Freitas |
| 1944 - Earl Sheely | Joe Marty | 1956 - Tommy Heath |
| | | 1957 - Tommy Heath |

## SAN DIEGO

| | | |
|---|---|---|
| 1938 - Frank Shellenback | 1946 - Pepper Martin | 1953 - Lefty O'Doul |
| 1939 - Cedric Durst | 1947 - Rip Collins | 1954 - Lefty O'Doul |
| 1940 - Cedric Durst | 1948 - Rip Collins | 1955 - Bob Elliott |
| 1941 - Cedric Durst | Jim Brillheart | 1956 - Bob Elliott |
| 1942 - Cedric Durst | 1949 - Bucky Harris | 1957 - Bob Elliott |
| 1943 - Cedric Durst | 1950 - Del Baker | George Metkovich |
| 1944 - George Detore | 1951 - Del Baker | |
| 1945 - Pepper Martin | 1952 - Lefty O'Doul | |

## SAN FRANCISCO

| | | |
|---|---|---|
| 1938 - Lefty O'Doul | 1945 - Lefty O'Doul | 1952 - Tommy Heath |
| 1939 - Lefty O'Doul | 1946 - Lefty O'Doul | 1953 - Tommy Heath |
| 1940 - Lefty O'Doul | 1947 - Lefty O'Doul | 1954 - Tommy Heath |
| 1941 - Lefty O'Doul | 1948 - Lefty O'Doul | 1955 - Tommy Heath |
| 1942 - Lefty O'Doul | 1949 - Lefty O'Doul | 1956 - Eddie Joost |
| 1943 - Lefty O'Doul | 1950 - Lefty O'Doul | Joe Gordon |
| 1944 - Lefty O'Doul | 1951 - Lefty O'Doul | 1957 - Joe Gordon |

## SEATTLE

| | | |
|---|---|---|
| 1938 - Jack Lelivelt | 1946 - Bill Skiff | 1953 - Bill Sweeney |
| 1939 - Jack Lelivelt | 1947 - Jo Jo White | 1954 - Jerry Priddy |
| 1940 - Jock Lelivelt | 1948 - Jo Jo White | 1955 - Fred Hutchinson |
| 1941 - Bill Skiff | 1949 - Jo Jo White | 1956 - Luke Sewell |
| 1942 - Bill Skiff | Bill Lawrence | Bill Brenner |
| 1943 - Bill Skiff | 1950 - Paul Richards | 1957 - Lefty O'Doul |
| 1944 - Bill Skiff | 1951 - Rogers Hornsby | |
| 1945 - Bill Skiff | 1952 - Bill Sweeney | |

## VANCOUVER

1956 - Lefty O'Doul
1957 - Charlie Metro

Lefty O'Doul and Bill Sweeney were the leading managers in terms of longevity. O'Doul managed all twenty years that I followed Coast League play. Sweeney managed 17 years, having missed only the 1942, 1947 and 1948 seasons. Ironically, no manager, including these two, won more than two league championships (1938–1957). Former Hollywood announcer Fred Haney managed only four years in the League and won twice, 1949 and 1952. The other multi-winner was Jack Lelivelt of Seattle. He won back-to-back pennants in 1939 and 1940. Technically, Bobby Bragan won two, as his 1954 Hollywood club ended in a tie with San Diego, but lost the playoff game. There were 68 different PCL managers from 1938 to 1957, including interim managers.

For seven straight years, Oakland had a playing manager, Johnny Vergez from 1939 through 1943, and Dolph Camilli in 1944 and 1945.

Manager Bill Skiff of Seattle is the one I liked best as a boy; this includes Hollywood managers. I was most impressed with him in the early years. As to why I should more vividly remember him as opposed to those who managed the two Los Angeles area teams, I can only say that the effective way he used his players made a strong impression on me. The departure of players to war forced Skiff to constantly change his lineup. I felt as a boy and still believe today that his success at putting players in the right positions was the result of wisdom, not luck.

# PACIFIC COAST LEAGUE CHAMPIONS 1938–1957

| YEAR | TEAM | MANAGER | WON | LOST | PCT. |
|------|------|---------|-----|------|------|
| 1938 | Los Angeles | Truck Hannah | 105 | 73 | .590 |
| 1939 | Seattle | Jack Lelivelt | 101 | 73 | .580 |
| 1940 | Seattle | Jack Lelivelt | 112 | 66 | .629 |
| 1941 | Seattle | Bill Skiff | 104 | 70 | .598 |
| 1942 | Sacramento | Pepper Martin | 105 | 73 | .590 |
| 1943 | Los Angeles | Bill Sweeney | 110 | 45 | .710 |
| 1944 | Los Angeles | Bill Sweeney | 99 | 70 | .586 |

| 1945 | Portland | Marvin Owen | 112 | 68 | .622 |
|------|----------|-------------|-----|----|------|
| 1946 | San Francisco | Lefty O'Doul | 115 | 68 | .628 |
| 1947 | Los Angeles | Bill Kelly | 106 | 81 | .567 |
| 1948 | Oakland | Casey Stengel | 114 | 74 | .606 |
| 1949 | Hollywood | Fred Haney | 109 | 78 | .583 |
| 1950 | Oakland | Charlie Dressen | 118 | 82 | .590 |
| 1951 | Seattle | Rogers Hornsby | 99 | 68 | .593 |
| 1952 | Hollywood | Fred Haney | 109 | 71 | .666 |
| 1953 | Hollywood | Bobby Bragan | 106 | 74 | .589 |
| 1954 | San Diego | Lefty O'Doul | 102 | 67 | .604 |
| 1955 | Seattle | Fred Hutchinson | 95 | 77 | .552 |
| 1956 | Los Angeles | Bob Sheffing | 107 | 61 | .637 |
| 1957 | San Francisco | Joe Gordon | 101 | 67 | .601 |

Los Angeles and Seattle tied for most championships won, each winning five. All eight League teams won at least one championship from 1938 to 1955.

Bill Sweeney's 1943 Los Angeles Angels had the best percentage, .710. They won 110 and lost only 45.

The 1955 Seattle Rainiers, under Fred Hutchinson, had the lowest percentage for a championship team, .552. They won 95 and lost 77. Only three championship teams won fewer than 100 games: Los Angeles in 1944 (99–70), Seattle in 1951 (99–68), and Seattle in 1955 (95–77).

# PACIFIC COAST LEAGUE PLAYOFFS

It should be noted that the Pacific Coast League has, in the course of its history, held a four-team playoff. The playoffs were first known as "The President's Cup Series." From 1944 on, it was called "The Governor's Cup Series." The playoff system first began in 1936. According to PCL records, the percentage champion was always listed and remained the League champion even when a non-pennant winner won the playoffs, hence these records will not be given. There were six years when no playoffs were held—1950, 1952, 1953, 1955, 1956 and 1957.

# PACIFIC COAST LEAGUE
# BATTING CHAMPIONS
# 1938–1957

| YEAR | NAME | BATTED | TEAM | AVG. | GAMES |
|------|------|--------|------|------|-------|
| 1938 | Frenchy Uhalt* | L | Hollywood | .332 | 166 |
| | Smead Jolley* | L | Hollywood/Oakland | .350 | 119 |
| 1939 | Dom Dallesandro | L | San Diego | .368 | 157 |
| 1940 | Lou Novikoff | R | Los Angeles | .363 | 174 |
| 1941 | John Moore | L | Los Angeles | .331 | 134 |
| 1942 | Ted Norbert | R | Portland | .378 | 149 |
| 1943 | Andy Pafko | R | Los Angeles | .356 | 157 |
| 1944 | Les Scarsella | L | Oakland | .328 | 156 |
| 1945 | Jo Jo White | L | Sacramento | .355 | 177 |
| 1946 | Harvey Storey | R | LA/Portland | .326 | 157 |
| 1947 | Hillis Layne | L | Seattle | .367 | 138 |
| 1948 | Gene Woodling | L | San Francisco | .385 | 146 |
| 1949 | Artie Wilson | L | San Diego/Oakland | .348 | 165 |
| 1950 | Frank Baumholtz | L | Los Angeles | .379 | 172 |
| 1951 | Jim Rivera | L | Seattle | .352 | 166 |
| 1952 | Bob Boyd | L | Seattle | .320 | 161 |
| 1953 | Bob Dillinger | R | Sacramento | .366 | 171 |
| 1954 | Harry Elliott | R | San Diego | .350 | 168 |
| 1955 | George Metkovich | L | Oakland | .335 | 151 |
| 1956 | Steve Bilko | R | Los Angeles | .360 | 162 |
| 1957 | Ken Aspromonte | R | San Francisco | .334 | 143 |

*Both men were awarded the 1938 batting title by different sources

Considering the fact that there were so many "career players" in the PCL, it is interesting to note that no player repeated as batting champion from 1938 through 1957. Over this twenty-year period, thirteen were left-handed batters, including Jolley; eight batted right-handed. For six straight years (1947–1952), left-handed batters won the title. Jo Jo White played the most games, 177 in 1945. Gene Woodling, in 1948, had the highest batting average, .385; Bob Boyd, in 1952, had the lowest average, .320.

# THE GREAT BATTLE
# FOR THE BATTING CROWN

The season of 1944 saw the closest battle for the League batting crown that I personally remember. It involved two favorites of mine, first baseman Les Scarsella of Oakland, and outfielder Frank Kelleher of Hollywood. Scarsella batted .32886; Kelleher, .32854. Perhaps it turned out as it should have. Scarsella came to bat 109 more times than Kelleher and played in 26 more games. Kelleher did, however, make the most of his at bats in the great battle of 1944, easily out-homering Scarsella. He also nudged him in RBI's. Kelleher being the long-ball hitter that he was, paid the price by striking out 58 times. Scarsella went down on strikes only 31 times. Both batters gained respect in the base-on-balls department. Kelleher walked 69 times, while Scarsella drew 45 free passes.

# PACIFIC COAST LEAGUE
# STADIUMS

Varying seating capacities involving several stadiums were recorded. The figures believed to be the most accurate are given.

**HOLLYWOOD**
1938 – Wrigley Field. Seating capacity 25,000
1939-1957 – Gilmore Field. Seating capacity 11,200

**LOS ANGELES**
1938-1957 – Wrigley Field. Seating capacity 25,000

**OAKLAND**
1938-1955 – Oaks Park. Seating capacity 11,000

**PORTLAND**
1938-1943 – Vaughn Street Park. Seating Capacity 12,000
1944-1955 – Lucky Beaver Stadium. Seating Capacity 12,500
1956-1957 – Multnomah Stadium. Seating Capacity 28,870

**SACRAMENTO**
1938-1943 – Cardinal Field. Seating Capacity 11,000
1944-1945 – Doubleday Park. Seating Capacity 11,000
1946-1957 – Edmonds Field. Seating Capacity 11,000

**SAN DIEGO**
1938-1957 – Lane Field. Seating Capacity 12,000

**SAN FRANCISCO**
1938-1957 – Seals' Stadium. Seating Capacity 25,000

**SEATTLE**
1938 – Sick's Rainier Park. Seating Capacity 15,000
1939-1949 – Sick's Seattle Stadium. Seating Capacity 15,000
1950-1957 – Sick's Stadium. Seating Capacity 15,000

**VANCOUVER**
1956-1957 – Capilano Stadium. Seating Capacity 9,200

I do not know for certain, but suspect that the stadiums in Sacramento, Seattle and Portland (Vaughn Street Park, Lucky Beaver Stadium) were not separate parks, but merely underwent name changes and also added more seats (Lucky Beaver Stadium).

# HOMES AWAY FROM HOME

The following is a list of hotels where PCL players stayed while on the road:

| HOLLYWOOD | LOS ANGELES | SACRAMENTO |
|---|---|---|
| Knickerbocker | Mayfair | Clunie |
| Roosevelt | Commodore | Senator |

| OAKLAND | SAN DIEGO | SEATTLE |
|---|---|---|
| Leamington | U.S. Grant | Olympic |

| SAN FRANCISCO | PORTLAND | VANCOUVER |
|---|---|---|
| Taylor | Imperial | Sylvia |
| Alexander Hamilton | Benson | |

Over the years, I have stayed in the following hotels: Leamington, Senator, U.S. Grant and the Alexander Hamilton.

# PCL FIELD DIMENSIONS

One of the most amazing features of baseball is its total inconsistency when it comes to fence distances and foul territory. True as this is, I doubt that any of us who love the game would want it any other way. I do, however, admit that I've often wondered why, somewhere along the line, fixed dimensions have not been established which would make the keeping of stats more accurate and fair. Although I accept this wacky part of the game, I do grow weary of the oft-repeated line used by even the most highly respected radio and television announcers, that goes something like this: "That home run just hit by 'Long Ball' Larry here at Super Star Stadium would just be a 'can of corn' at Pleasurable Podunk Park."

Well, the old Coast League parks were no exception when it came to odd fence distances. Quite frankly, I have no recollection of the few Coast League announcers that I knew about ever wearing out the tired cliche such as I mentioned above. No Hollywood announcer ever had anything to say about it to my knowledge. It was simply accepted as part of the game. Speaking of announcers, Bud Foster of Oakland and the late Leo Lassen of Seattle were two outstanding PCL announcers that I personally knew of. I often picked up Lassen late at night in Southern California over station KOMO.

Here are the dimensions of the ten PCL parks:

**HOLLYWOOD**
Gilmore Field
Left field – 335'
Center field – 400'
Right field – 335'

**LOS ANGELES**
Wrigley Field
Left field – 340'
Center field – 412'
Right field – 339'

**OAKLAND**
Oaks Park
Left field – 335'
Center field – 395'
Right field – 300'

**PORTLAND**
Lucky Beaver Stadium
Left field – 331'
Center field – 368'
Right field – 315'

**PORTLAND**
Multnomah Stadium
Left field – 305'
Center field – 412'
Right field – 340'

**SACRAMENTO**
Edmonds Field
Left field – 326'
Center field – 452'
Right field – 326'

**SAN DIEGO**
Lane Field
Left field – 330'
Center field – 452'
Right field – 329'

**SAN FRANCISCO**
Seals' Stadium
Left field – 365'
Center field – 404'
Right field – 350'

**SEATTLE**
Sick's Stadium
Left field – 335'
Center field – 415'
Right field – 335'

**VANCOUVER**
Capilano Stadium
Left field – 335'
Center field – 415'
Right field – 335'

Of these ten parks, only four were symmetrical. San Diego and Sacramento had the longest distance to straightaway center field – 452'. Portland's Lucky Beaver Stadium had the shortest – 368'. San Francisco boasted the longest distance to left field (365') and also the longest distance to right field (350'). Portland's Multnomah Stadium had the shortest distance to left field – 305' (another football stadium). Oakland had the shortest right field fence – 300'.

Because of the long distance to straightaway center field at Los Angeles (412'), I remember the batting cage was always left against the center field wall in the field of play. It was, of course, folded up. Continuing some additional thoughts regarding Wrigley Field, as you can see from the listed fence dimensions only San Francisco's left field fence was deeper than that of Wrigley Field. Still, in the minds of most of us fans, Wrigley's left field wall played shorter than most PCL parks. The ball carried extremely well to left field. Don't hold me to it, but I believe more home runs were hit out of Wrigley Field during the years the American League's Los Angeles Angels played there than any other AL stadium.

# RECORDS AND STATS

**ATTENDANCE RECORDS:**

Highest Attendance Season League Total: 4,068,432 – 1947
Highest Season Attendance Club: San Francisco, 670,563 – 1946
Highest Attendance Single Game:
23,603, Oakland at San Francisco – July 30, 1946
Highest Attendance Double Header:
23,090, San Diego at Los Angeles – May 15, 1949
Highest Attendance Day/Night Double Header:
Sacramento at Portland – April 27, 1956
Day Game ................................... 16,929
Night game ................................ 17,521
Total Attendance ........................ 34,450

From a League high of 4,068,432 in 1947, PCL attendance began to fall off, reaching a low of 1,635,526 in 1956, after hovering around the 1.7 million mark the previous three years. This decline could perhaps be attributed to the fact that some teams were televising local contests. Television, in general, could also have contributed. The feeling, particularly around 1956 and 1957, that certain teams were in a lame-duck situation might also have been a factor. One thing I will never admit is that the high caliber of baseball declined. All the ingredients that brought about success at the gate in previous years were still operative right up to and including 1957.

**PITCHING RECORDS:**

Most Strike-Outs Lifetime:
1,866 – "Kewpie Dick" Barrett from 1935 to 1950
Most Consecutive Innings No Base on Balls:
66⅔ – George Bamberger, Vancouver
Most Games Won:
295 – Frank Shellenback, 1920 to 1937.*
Most Hit Batsmen One Game:
4 – Charlie Gassaway, Oakland vs. San Francisco, May 14, 1950
Most Innings Pitched: 4,185 – Frank Shellenback

---

*All of these brief records involved players who appeared during my years as a PCL fan. Frank Shellenback qualifies, since he appeared as a manager in 1938 (San Diego).

# RECORDS AND STATZ

All of the following PCL records belong to "Jigger" Statz:

| | |
|---|---:|
| Most games played | 2,790 |
| Most at bats | 10,657 |
| Most total bases | 4,405 |
| Most hits | 3,356 |
| Most doubles | 595 |
| Most triples | 137 |
| Most runs scored | 1,996 |
| Most put-outs | 6,872 |
| Most years with one team (Los Angeles) | 18 |

Most Games Won in Relief One Season:
    20 – Leo Kiely, San Francisco, 1957
Most Consecutive Games Won in Relief:
    14 – Leo Kiely, San Francisco, April 14–July 21, 1957

# SEVEN WINNINGEST PITCHERS 1938–1957

| | WON | LOST | PCT. |
|---|---|---|---|
| Frank Shellenback | 295 | 178 | .624 |
| "Kewpie Dick" Barrett | 234 | 168 | .582 |
| Tony Freitas | 228 | 175 | .566 |
| Sam Gibson | 227 | 140 | .619 |
| Herm Pillette | 226 | 235 | .491 |
| Jack Salveson | 204 | 166 | .551 |
| Hal Turpin | 203 | 158 | .562 |

Tony Freitas was the winningest left-handed pitcher in the minor leagues. He won 112 games in minor league circuits, other than the PCL.

# NO-HITTERS

Without question, the pitching of a no-hitter is one of the most exciting accomplishments in baseball. A sparkling fielding play, a little luck and good "stuff" on the part of the pitcher involved all go into the making of a no-hitter, and add greatly to the excitement. Most of us who have followed the game for any length of time have observed a no-hitter either in person or by way of radio or television. I'm sure we all agree there is little to compare with the tension and mounting pressure we feel when one of these games builds to its climax. Even fans on the losing side exult with a pitcher who has just thrown a no-hitter. Much to my disappointment, I never saw or heard a no-hitter in the PCL, but have in subsequent years experienced the thrill. It is something that one never forgets.

There were 25 no-hitters tossed by 23 different pitchers from 1938 through 1957 in the PCL. They are as follows:

**1938**    **Joe Berry** of Los Angeles against Oakland
           July 10: 4 to 0 – 7 innings
           **Dick Ward** of San Diego against Los Angeles
           Aug. 30: 1 to 0
                     Ward pitched 12⅔ innings before giving up a hit.
                     The game lasted 16 innings and he allowed just 2 hits.

**1939, 1940, 1941**   None

**1942**    **Hal Turpin** of Seattle against San Diego
           April 12: 2 to 0

**1943**    **Cotton Pippin** of Oakland against Sacramento
           May 31 : 10 to 0 – Perfect game, 7 innings
                     Pippen threw only 64 pitches

**1944**    **George Cornellas** of Los Angeles against San Francisco
           May 7: 2 to 0
           **Manny Salvo** of Oakland against Sacramento
           July 19: 2 to 0

**1945**    None

**1946**    **Joe Demoran** of Seattle against Los Angeles
           April 4: 3 to 0
           **Ad Liska** of Portland against Hollywood
           April 21: 1 to 0 – 7 innings
           **Garth "Red" Mann** of Sacramento against Seattle
           May 31: 6 to 0

**1947**    **Tommy Bridges** of Portland against San Francisco
April 20: 2 to 0

**1948**    **"Kewpie Dick"** Barrett of Seattle against Sacramento
May 15: 3 to 0 – Perfect game, 7 innings

**1949, 1950**   None

**1951**    **Paul Culvert** of Seattle against Sacramento
May 27: 4 to 0
**Warren Hacker** of Los Angeles against Seattle
Sept. 7: 4 to 0

**1952**    **Elmer Singleton** of San Francisco against Sacramento
April 24: 12⅓ innings
> Singleton lost the game in the 13th inning 1 to 0 on 3 hits.

**Harold Gregg** of Oakland against Portland
May 1: 3 to 0 – 7 innings
**Roger Bowman** of Oakland against Hollywood.
July 3: 5 to 0

**1953**    **Joe Hatten** of Los Angeles against Son Diego
June 7: 6 to 0 – 7 innings
**Red Munger** of Hollywood against Sacramento
July 4: 1 to 0 – 7 innings
**Jim Atkins** of Oakland against San Francisco
Aug. 25: 2 to 0 – 7 innings

**1954**    **Bubba Church** of Los Angeles against Portland
Aug. 3: 3 to 0
**Bob Alexander** of Portland against Oakland
Aug. 17: 3 to 0 – 7 innings
**Roger Bowman** of Hollywood against Portland
Sept. 12: 10 to 0 – Perfect game, 7 innings

**1955**    **George Piktuzis** of Los Angeles against San Francisco
July 21: 2 to 1
**Elmer Singleton** of Seattle against San Diego
July 24: 2 to 0 – 7 innings
**Chris Van Cuyk** of Oakland against Los Angeles
July 26: 2 to 0 – 7 innings

**1956, 1957**   None

Of this list of no-hit pitchers, Roger Bowman and Elmer Singleton achieved the feat twice. Bowman's second gem was a perfecto. It came in game two of a double-header on the closing day of the 1954 season. This victory enabled Hollywood to tie San Diego for the League championship and was a most gratifying victory for Bowman.

To illustrate how things so quickly change, Bobby Bragan started Bowman in Saturday's game, and he gave up four successive base hits. Bragan immediately made a pitching change and came back with Roger in game two of the Sunday doubleheader; the rest is history. Bobby was praised for his quick and decisive move which enabled the Stars to keep alive their championship hopes. This great performance by Roger Bowman showed: eleven ground balls and eight strike outs. He was only in danger two times. Eddie Basinski hit a deep fly ball which was gathered in by Dale Long. The last threat came in the bottom of the seventh when Dino Restelli, seeing Jack Phillips playing deep at third, attempted to lay down a bunt with two strikes and two outs. The ball trickled foul just short of the bag, sending Restelli down on strikes and sending Hollywood to San Diego for a one-game playoff.

# THE BOWMAN NO-HIT YEARS

Date of first no-hitter: July 3, 1952

| GAMES | WON | LOST | PCT. | SO | BB | ERA |
|-------|-----|------|------|----|----|-----|
| 17 | 7 | 5 | .583 | 65 | 31 | 3.28 |

Date of second no-hitter:
          September 12, 1954 — Perfect Game (7 innings)

| GAMES | WON | LOST | PCT. | SO | BB | ERA |
|-------|-----|------|------|----|----|-----|
| 46 | 22 | 13 | .629 | 165 | 99 | 2.51 |

Bowman's 2.51 ERA was 7th best in the League. His 6 shutouts were second best. Eddie Erautt of San Diego blanked the opposition seven times. Bowman played for three PCL teams — Oakland, Hollywood and Sacramento.

Los Angeles was involved in the most no-hit games—nine. They won six and lost three. Oakland played in eight, winning six and losing two. Sacramento played in seven and went two and five. All of the eight teams (Vancouver not included) participated in no-hit games., San Francisco was the only, team

that did not win at least one game. They were 0 and 5. This includes the no-hitter (12⅓ innings) by Elmer Singleton in 1952, which he ultimately lost in 13 innings to Sacramento.

# THE RELIEF PITCHER

My Uncle Rube Stadler, a former semi-pro baseball player now in his 80's, was one of those who was fortunate enough to see the great Walter Johnson pitch, as well as other outstanding pitchers from yesteryear. In talking with him about pitching in those days, he emphasized the fact that pitchers always went the full 9, even extra innings when necessary. It is a fact that the Coast League had a 24-inning game where both pitchers went all the way. Even though there is much gray hair in my beard, which is very noticeable when I fail to use Mr. Gillette's invention regularly, the relief pitcher was in evidence in my Coast League days. He has, however, undergone a metamorphosis. I recall the Coast League reliever in my time as not really being a specialist, but one who came by the job primarily because he was somewhat older than most starting pitchers. In a sense he could be called a specialist because the years have certainly given him pitching savvy. He was nonetheless not specifically groomed for the task. With the expected exceptions, this was the relief method used in the PCL.

Let me tell you of another kind of relief pitcher who saw action in the PCL. He was for sure not specifically groomed for the task, did not possess too much pitching savvy, or was necessarily older. This "pitcher" was a mop-up man, and most often a utility player who would be brought in after the outcome of the game had already been decided. Infielder "Lucky" Jack Lohrke was one such individual used in hopeless games. I've seen him summoned for mound duty on three or four occasions.

Well, today we see pitchers regularly being groomed to spend their entire careers in relief. The more rubber-armed individuals take the long relief stints, while the hard throwers come into the fray in the latter innings, especially if the score is tied or their team has the lead.

As regards percentage baseball, although it has always been around, it's my belief that we are seeing much more of it now than in days gone by. I personally am not 100% sold on it.*

## THE FESLER EXPERIMENT

If you have ever played the game of softball, or followed it closely, you know that a talented, overpowering softball pitcher is extremely difficult, if not impossible to hit. The natural upward trajectory of the ball, the pitcher's ability to also make the ball sink, along with the accelerated speed of a sphere coming toward you from only 46 feet away, all prove my point. Having personally had more experience playing softball as opposed to baseball, believe me, I have had many moments of frustration facing some of these overwhelming pitchers.

One such super-talented softball hurler who sent opposing batters back to the bench muttering to themselves was Bob Fesler of Seattle, Washington. He had over 150 no-hitters to his credit. Fred Hutchinson, who piloted the Seattle Rainiers in 1955, became interested in Fesler, especially after seeing him strike out 11 Seattle and Sacramento batters in an exhibition game from the normal softball distance of 46 feet. Fred, himself a former great

---

*In a game in the early '50s, Fred Haney brought left-hander Paul Pettit in to pitch to the left-hand hitting Joe Brovia. Brovia delivered a shot off the right center field wall Haney purposely passed a right-handed batter to get to Brovia.

pitcher, believed Fesler could be a successful baseball pitcher using his own delivery, but of course pitching from 60 feet away. Seattle management agreed and signed Fesler to a contract during the '55 season.

I wish I could tell you that all went well for Fesler, but such was not the case. His failure to succeed was almost entirely due to lack of control. I never saw him pitch, but listened to one of his games on the radio. I felt sorry for him as one by one opposing batters reached first base via the base on balls. Needless to say, he was soon out of the game, and all too quickly the interesting experiment came to an end. The added 14 feet from mound to home plate was too great, and it negated Fesler's effectiveness, which was unbelievable from the normal softball distance. Bob appeared in only four games and had a record of 0 and 2.

Should the thought have crossed your mind that Hutchinson encouraged Seattle management to sign Fesler strictly as a gimmick, I feel absolutely certain that he had no such thought. Bear in mind that Seattle was involved in a battle for the pennant which involved no fewer than four teams. The Rainiers ultimately won the crown by three games. This they did in spite of Bob Fesler. Hutch believed they could win it with his help. Only four games separated the fourth-place Angels from Seattle. It was an interesting and tough race right down to the end.*

No, Fred Hutchinson did not engage in any foolishness, and my hat is off to him for giving Bob Fesler the opportunity to become a professional baseball pitcher. Fesler, too, is to be commended for accepting the challenge. This experiment, though unsuccessful, was just another reason why the Coast League was so tremendously exciting to follow.

# CIRCUIT STEW

If you survived the *Horsehide Hash* we had earlier, I hope you won't mind a little *Circuit Stew*. I'm going to serve you some bits

---

*Hollywood and Los Angeles ended in a third-place tie, each winning 91 and losing 81. The Stars defeated the Angels in a playoff three games to two, thus making L.A. the fourth-place team.

and bites of some things that took place in the League from my first year of 1938 through 1957. We'll have a morsel or two to give you for most, but not every year. By the way, if you should get indigestion anytime during the meal, please turn back to page 40. Just over Frenchy Uhalt's left shoulder, you'll see a bottle of Bromo Seltzer on the left field wall. Stir two teaspoons of its magic crystals in a glass of water; you'll feel better. Oh, don't forget to put the cap back on. (Incidentally, any batter who hit the Bromo Seltzer bottle back in 1939 received $10.)

* * * * *

San Francisco, with a team batting average of .292, led the League in team batting in 1938. The Angels were second with an average of .284. No less than six Angels hit over .300, which played a major part in leading L.A. to the pennant. Sacramento had the distinction of having the lowest team batting average, .250. The Solons did, however, show some muscle by hitting 121 home runs, which led the League.

There were two PCL batting champions named in 1938. I have found two sets of records. One source gives the title to Frenchy Uhalt, while the other gives it to Smead Jolley. Although Jolley had a higher batting average, .350 to Uhalt's .332, he appeared in 47 fewer games and came to bat 221 fewer times. This doubtless accounted for the one statistician givng the nod to Uhalt.

* * * * *

As early as 1939 it was evident that Lefty O'Doul was a good judge of major league prospects. He was credited with sending outfielder Dom DiMaggio and pitcher Lawrence Powell to the majors. DiMaggio hit .360, with 14 home runs and 82 RBI's. Powell was 12 and 11 with the Seals, but his 2.79 ERA was seventh best in the league. Regarding Dom DiMaggio, although overshadowed by brother Joe, he was an outstanding major league player year in and year out. The PCL was well known for those it sent to the big leagues; Dom DiMaggio was far from the least of these.

Gilmore Field opened for play in 1939. Although I have no figures, it was an excellent year at the turnstiles for Hollywood, and a super year for Seattle at the gate and on the field. Over 500,000 poured through the turnstiles at Sick's Seattle Stadium.

After the Angels had run off 19 straight victories, it looked impossible for any team to overtake them, but Seattle and San Francisco did. When the dust had settled, the Angels finished in third place six games behind Seattle in the lost column and one game behind San Francisco.

* * * * *

In 1940, "Kewpie Dick" Barrett won 24 games for Seattle. He, along with the outstanding play of Billy Schuster and Al Niemiec, helped put the Sick's Seattle Stadium gang out of sight. That year they finished ten games ahead of second-place Los Angeles.

* * * * *

Nineteen-forty-one saw the inauguration of the first PCL All-star Game. It was held in Seals' Stadium in San Francisco. The final score: South – 3, North – 1. There were several years when all-star games were not held. The highest all-star game attendance that I have record of was in 1948: 14,212. The lowest was in 1955: 3,204.

* * * * *

The war years of 1942 through 1945 saw baseball continue in the PCL. A normal playing schedule was maintained throughout the war. "Kewpie Dick" Barrett, Alpha Brazle, Clem Drieswerd and Bob Joyce were the earned run leaders among PCL pitchers from 1942 to 1945 in the order listed.

In 1942, on the last day of the season Sacramento, needing a double-header victory over the League-leading Angels to win the pennant, got it. Clarence Beers won the first game 7-to-5, with two innings of relief help from Tony Freitas. Freitas came right back in game two and beat the Angels 5-to-1, going all the way (7 innings).

Billy Raimondi played all nine positions in the last game of the 1943 season.

* * * * *

In 1946, San Francisco beat out neighbor Oakland for the pennant in a close race. San Francisco set an all-time attendance mark that year. Because of the tight race between the two Bay

Area teams, San Francisco also set a record for a single game on July 30 against the Oaks. Hollywood led in team batting, .261, and home runs, 92. The champion San Francisco Seals hit only 32 home runs, the fewest, but led in RBI's, 714. San Diego had the fewest RBI's, 568, and lowest team batting average, .247.

\* \* \* \* \*

In 1947, San Francisco and Los Angeles ended in a tie, each winning 105 and losing 81. Los Angeles defeated the Seals 5 to 0 to claim the title. This loss denied Lefty O'Doul his third PCL championship during my time.

Bud Beasley, one of many PCL clowns, was actually traded because of one caper. He was brought in by Sacramento skipper Dick Bartell to pitch to Lou Novikoff and warned that he would be fined $100 if he pitched the slugger above the waist. Bud complied by winding up and rolling the ball to the plate. Next stop, Seattle.\*

Nineteen-forty-eight saw old Casey Stengel lead Oakland to the League crown, and in the process be named Manager of the Year. While speaking of Casey Stengel, and since you may have expected me to have remembered some humorous incidents concerning Casey when he managed at Oakland, I must admit I can give you none. I sincerely believe his "Stengeleze" and interesting mannerisms really came to the fore after he became the manager of the Yankees. If you want a short story on him, my buddy Rich Timmis told me that he had it on good authority that Stengel, while managing the Yanks, would quite often drift off to sleep during the course of the game. His coaches would carry on his duties and inform him of the outcome at the game's conclusion. So much for one Casey Stengel.

Padre outfielder/first baseman Jack Graham, appearing to be on his way to breaking Tony Lazzeri's mark of 60 home runs in a season, was beaned on July 25. He already had hit 46 homers. He appeared in only 21 more games and tacked on just two more round-trippers, finishing with a total of 48. To finish off the '40s, old Portland favorite Ad Liska, at the age of 42, won only four games in 1949. Oddly, all of Liska's victories were against Oakland.

---

\*PCL funny men never rated themselves to my knowledge with the exception of Bud Beasley. Bud considered himself to be the Clown Prince of the Coast League.

* * * * *

In 1950, Oakland captured the title, winning 118 games, the most victories for a pennant winner between 1938 and 1957. They lost 82 games, the most losses for a championship team between the same years. Imagine a 200-game schedule! Earl Rapp hit .347, with 24 home runs and 145 RBI's. Al Gettel won 23 and lost 7. The Oaks led in team batting, .289. SOME TEAM!

* * * * *

In 1951, Joe Gordon became playing manager of Sacramento. He led the League in home runs (43) and RBI's (136), three more than runner-up Joe Brovia.

The year of 1952 was the year Open Classification came to the PCL. This classification was designed to bring about the eventual major league status of the League.*

Milo Candini, appearing in 69 games, set a PCL record for appearances in relief. He started only one game. This was a rewarding year for the 35-year-old Oakland pitcher who hooked on with the Oaks one month into the season.

* * * * *

Nineteen-fifty-three saw pitcher Tony Ponce bring pitching magic to the Coast League. He started the season in the low minors and proceeded to lose 20 games. He nonetheless was called up to San Francisco late in the season, where he made the most of his opportunity. He won eight straight games and did not taste defeat. In defense of Tony as regards his poor showing in the Class-C California League, he was on a last place team, which doubtless had something to do with his losing 20 games.

This year also marked the 50th birthday of the Pacific Coast League. As expected, there were numerous ceremonies in commemoration of this memorable year. Many oldtimers' games were held all over the League.

* * * * *

---

*OPEN CLASSIFICATION was a multifaceted plan. It, in part, banned working agreements with major league teams, banned the use of players on option from the majors and required waivers to sell a player back to the organization from which he was acquired.

In 1954, a most unusual thing happened: a protest was upheld by League President "Pants" Rowland. Seattle protested a game with Sacramento and won. The game was thrown out. I don't have any information on what brought on the protest. The pitchers' victory and defeat were not allowed on the record. All other individuals and team records were allowed to stand.

This year marked the second time two teams finished in a tie during my time. This season it involved San Diego and Hollywood. San Diego won the playoff game in Lane Field 7 to 2 on the afternoon of September 13. After missing Roger Bowman's memorable no-hitter to give Hollywood a tie, I was determined to see them win the playoff game. I journeyed to San Diego for that game and came home very disappointed. In spite of my disappointment, I can tell you this was a super year for the Stars, and of course San Diego, but not for the rest of the League. Third-place Oakland finished 16 games behind Hollywood and 17 behind Lefty O'Doul's champion Padres.

\* \* \* \* \*

The 1956 season saw the now Vancouver manager, Lefty O'Doul, insert himself into the lineup as a pinch hitter. He hit a Gene Bearden pitch for a triple. The unusual thing about that was that he was 59 years old at the time. I understand that Sacramento manager Tommy Heath moved his outfielders in, thus making it easier for the former National League Batting Champ. It was still a feat that deserves mention.

\* \* \* \* \*

As we slowly run out of stew, let me tell you about the Angels' home run explosion of 1957. They tied a PCL record by hitting nine home runs in one game. All nine round-trippers were hit off of Sacramento hurler Roger Osenbaugh. One year earlier Heath showed a little kindness to Lefty O'Doul but he sure let Roger Osenbaugh suffer in this game against the Angels. Bert Hamric had three homers, two in the same inning; Jim Fridley one; Sparky Anderson one—a grand-slammer; Tommy Saffell one; Bobby Dolan one; Steve Bilko and Jim Baxes one each. The final score was 22 to 5. Don't tell anyone, but Osenbaugh broke curfew the night before.

With a big assist from Steve Bilko, the Angels led the League in home runs, hitting 167.

# WARTIME BASEBALL
# IN THE PCL

Being born and raised in Santa Monica, California meant that as a boy and teenager I was close to the wartime effort. Not far from my home stood the Douglas aircraft plant, which built the A-20 light bomber and employed somewhere between 30,000 and 40,000 at its peak years. Across the street from our old home, in the Ocean Park section of the city, was one of many small army camps. On these sites were located helium-filled barrage balloons. These balloons were connected to a cable and elevated by use of a winch. Their purpose was to ensnare enemy aircraft which might be sent to destroy Douglas aircraft. Fortunately for us, this never happened.

Needless to say, fears and anxieties ran high for people of all ages during thse years. The need for diversion in the form of entertainment was absolutely necessary here, as it was in your hometown. Many of the big bands appeared at the old Casino Gardens on the Ocean Front. Western bands performed on the old Venice Pier. Many of these bands were available for the different shifts at the Douglas plant. Swing-shift dances were the most popular of all. Overflow crowds were the norm.

As many of you know, most every city in the Pacific Coast League was heavily involved in the war effort. As an additional diversion for the war worker, PCL baseball continued a normal schedule during the years of 1942 to 1945. I truly believe this was a wise decision, all things being considered. With the younger players gone to war, the preponderance of those playing in the League were the "older" men. We also saw the use of some "kid" players.

Two such youngsters who immediately come to mind are Bill Sami, a catcher with the L.A. Angels, and Vic Picetti, a left-handed first baseman who played with Oakland. I canÆt say for sure, but Sarni was probably the youngest of the young, being no

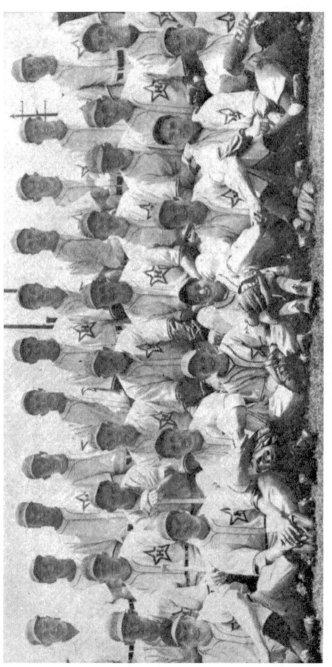

**HOLLYWOOD BASEBALL CLUB – 1944 SEASON**

Top Row, Left to Right: Dr. Meekle, Krug, coach; Intlekofer, Sharp, Olsen, Weldon, Clements, Kelleher, Powers, Embree, Younker.
Second Row: Babe Herman, Hill, Moran, Holder, Mgr. Charlie Root, Richardson, Hufford, Wilson, Mishasek, Goldsberry.
Bottom Row: Mestele, Escalante, Smith, Bat Boy, Mascot Sandy Oster, Davis, Gonzales, Jones.

**LOS ANGELES BASEBALL CLUB – 1944 SEASON**

Front Row, Left to Right: Grigg, c; Miller, ss; Willingham, utility if; Ostrowski, of; Fernandes, c; Garriott, of; Stein, p.
Second Row: Cornellas, p; Moore, utility of; Adams, p; Sweeney, mgr.; English 3b; Sarni, c; Russell, 2b; Otero, 1 b.
Back Row: Toro, trainer; Gray, utility if; Smalley, ss; Phipps, p; Prim, p; Roger, p; Sauer, of; Osborn, p; Norbert, of.

**SAN FRANCISCO SEALS – 1945 SEASON**

Top Row, Left to Right: Joe Sprinz, c; Bob Joyce, p; Dick Wilson, c; John Perry, 3b; Frank Seward, p; Ken Brondel, p; Lefty O'Doul, mgr; Bones Sanders, 1b; Bob Barthelson, p; Ken Miller, p; Leo Hughes, trainer. Second Row: Bernie Uhalt, cf; B. Ogrodowski, c; Bill Enos, lf; Gus Suhr, lb; Neil Sheridan, rf; Ben Guintini, cf; Tony Buzolich, p; Knowles Piercey, p; H. Steinbacher, lf; Roy Nicely, ss; Del Young, 2b. Bottom Row; Red Burnham; Okey Flowers, p; Elmer Orella, p; John Trutta, 3b; Chas. Nelson, c; Ralph Watson, 2b; John Cavalli, 3b; Joe Futernick, ss; Emil Mailho, rf; Doug Oliver, p; Floyd Ehman, p.

more than 15 when he first put on an Angel uniform. Sarni played during the war, in 1943, '44 and '45, and again after the war in 1947. Picetti played in '44 and '45. Sarni eventually went to the majors in 1951. Picetti returned to the low minors and was killed in a minor league bus accident. It was this same bus that "Lucky" Jack Lohrke was on. Lohrke departed the bus earlier in the day, having been notified he was returning to the PCL.*

One of the "older" players that I remember as having played on a part-time basis was Hollywood outfielder Les Powers. He first played in 1944 and again in 1945. I remember him very well, since he taught at my high school in Santa Monica. Powers played only the home games until school was out, and then he joined the team on the road.**

Needless to say, there was much player movement as the many players changed from the baseball uniform to a military one. No doubt those in the "baseball know" will tell you we had sub-par baseball in the PCL during the war. Since I wasn't in the know, you couldn't prove it by me. I just went on enjoying the games and appreciating those men who gave us baseball during those dark days in our American history. I will tell you this: after going over the many pages of players' records, coupled with the memory of games I saw, it is my conviction that the League maintained a high quality of player personnel all throughout the war.

To validate this, allow me to list ten players who played at least three years during the war:

|                 |                |
|-----------------|----------------|
| Larry Barton    | Butch Moran    |
| Cecil Garriott  | Billy Raimondi |
| Brooks Holder   | Les Scarsella  |
| Bob Joyce       | Tom Seats      |
| Ad Liska        | Frenchy Uhalt  |

These men were not representative of the negative meaning attached to the words "Wartime Player." They played successfully before, during, and after the war. *No rookie coming up or*

---

*I could stand corrected, but very much believe that **Gordon Goldsberry**, a left-handed first baseman, was one of these "kid" players. He began with Hollywood in 1944 and eventually played with several PCL teams.

**Like Powers, **Chet Johnson** was a part-time player during the war. He worked in the Seattle shipyards and pitched only in home games.

*young ballplayer returning from the war forced them out of baseball;* Father Time, yes, but no one else. They were joined by other seasoned veterans and the relatively few youngsters in maintaining the high standards of Pacific Coast League baseball.

# ALL-PACIFIC RECREATION FUND

I'm certain there were many groups and organizations that provided for the recreational needs of our military men during the war, both at home and abroad. One such organization that was formed here in Los Angeles was the All-Pacific Recreation Fund. It was brought into being by the late, great comedian **Joe E. Brown**, who was conceded to be baseball's No. 1 fan. Brown was the APRF Chairman, which had on its board of directors 19 outstanding sports personages. Though originally formed for the purpose of sending equipment to the Pacific, it literally sent sports equipment to every front, thus being called All-Pacific Recreation Fund in name only. An incredible 97.9% of all monies raised went for equipment, while the remaining 2.1% went for expenses. Examples of the type of equipment sent are as follows:

> *Baseballs, baseball gloves, baseball bats, polo balls, medicine balls, softballs, volleyballs and nets, footballs, basketballs, fishing tackle, horseshoe sets, etc.*

In addition to the above, *The Sporting News* sent 6,000 weekly copies of their overseas edition for distribution in 1943.

Money for these items, and many more, was raised by the staging of a baseball game at Wrigley Field, Los Angeles. (There were two such games that I remember.) A combined team of players from Hollywood and Los Angeles went up against a servicemen's team called Service All-Stars, the majority of which played in the PCL before the war. There were also players on this team who were yet to play in the League after their major league careers were over.

No player from the three reams represented received money from the game. The Los Angeles Baseball Club donated Wrigley Field and its box office facilities free of charge. Even the directors

**JOE E. BROWN**

of the All-Pacific Recreation Fund purchased tickets. The official program was printed at a loss by the *Downtown Shopping News*. Someone wrote concerning the APRF that it was the closest thing to a 100% charity that was ever conceived. Over $20,000 was received from the first game, which was played in 1943.1 have no figures from the 1944 game, but it was expected that it brought in even a larger amount than the year before.

I remember attending one of those games (though I can't remember which one) with my long-time friend Ben Torres, who is now a college professor and successful businessman as well. I recall having the good feeling that we were a small part of a large undertaking that thoroughly succeeded in meeting the recreational needs of servicemen around the world.

I came into possession of a souvenir program from one of these games after I had completed my handwritten notes on *Wartime Baseball in the PCL*. It fully corroborates my feelings that it was a right and proper decision to allow baseball to continue during the war years. Servicemen stationed throughout the world gave their blessing to its continuance, as well as those of us at home.

# ROY SMALLEY MAKES GOOD

The progression through the low minors to the high minors is the process most players take to attain their coveted goal of eventually putting on a major league uniform. Some may have been fortunate enough to have begun somewhere in-between the low and the high. All, however, in order to reach the majors must have played the game well or showed sufficient potential or they could not expect a call to the big leagues. We, as fans, are not too often surprised when certain minor league players progress to the big time. Now and then, though, there are those whose minor league credentials seem to indicate anything but a call to the majors. One such player was Roy Smalley of the Los Angeles Angels. I'm extremely happy to relate his story as best I recall it, because things worked out so well for this man. I wish there were more stories that paralleled this one.

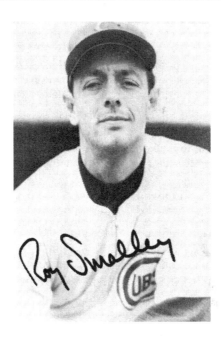

I first remember Smalley with the Angels in 1944. His batting average that year was .188. He appeared in 61 games. He was not with the Angels in 1945. I remember his being with L.A. in 1946, where he appeared in only nine games and batted .214. That same year he played for Shelby in the Tri-State League, where he hit .219, and Davenport in the Three-I League, where he played only briefly and had no batting average. Both of these leagues were, of course, lower in classification than the PCL. In 1947, he played at Des Moines, Iowa, in the Western League, where his batting average was .244. The Western League could not have been higher than Class A.

In 1948, he was given the opportunity to make the Chicago Cubs roster, and he emphatically did just that. Before anyone knew what happened, he became the regular shortstop of the Cubs, a position he was to hold for many years.

So anxious was I for this man to make good, I forgot that no Hollywood Star fan should have anything to do with anyone connected with the Angels, especially the parent Chicago Cubs. Nevertheless, Smalley became my favorite major leaguer throughout his entire big league career. The success of Smalley was most exciting to me and most rewarding to him.

I'm not going to tell you that Smalley set the majors on fire, but I can tell you he became a ten-year man. You've got to show something to stay up that long. Even Smalley's celebrated brother-in-law, Gene Mauch, can't show ten years of major league service as a player. Smalley played the last two or three years of his career with the Philadelphia Phillies before retiring in the mid-1950s.

And yes, the name of Smalley is still around. Roy Smalley III is a fine ballplayer and has already made his mark in the game. However, I never hear that name but what I think of Roy Smalley, Jr., the man that seemingly didn't belong, but since no one told him he hung around for ten years.

> *Did you know that the favorite dessert of PCL players was bundt cake?*

# LONGEVITY LIST
## (Partial/Unofficial)

**Herm Pillette** holds the PCL record for length of service as a player in the Coast League (23 years); this includes all positions. In spite of the fact that his pitching records show him to be under the 500 mark (226–235), his durability and longevity is absolutely worthy of special mention. He played for seven PCL teams between the years of 1920 and 1945. He closed his career with Sacramento in 1945, being a few months short of Birthday No. 48.

The following 30 players, managers, and coach appeared in the PCL for ten or more years. These are proof of what we mean by "career" PCL players. To further illustrate the point regarding length of PCL service, this list includes the years before and after 1938, but not beyond 1957.

YEARS

40  Jimmy Reese — Player and Coach

23  Herm Pillette

22  Truck Hannah — Player and Manager

20  Eddie Mulligan

20  Lefty O'Doul — At least 20 years as both player and Manager

20  Billy Raimondi

20  Frenchy Uhalt

19  Frank Shellenback — Player and Manager

18  Jigger Statz — All with Los Angeles as both Player and Manager

18  Hal Turpin

17  Bill Sweeney — At least 17 years as both Player and Manager

16  Tony Freitas — Player and Manager

15  Dick Gyselman — Played only third base in the PCL

14  Sam Gibson

14  Brooks Holder

14  Ad Liska — All with Portland

13  "Kewpie Dick" Barrett

13  Bill Lawrence — All with Seattle as both Player and Manager

12  Gene Handley

12  Frank Kelleher

12  Jack Salveson

11  Eddie Basinski

11  Joe Brovia

11  Al Lein

11  Gene Lillard

11  Ted Norbert

10  Larry Barton — Played 24 years in the minors, all at first base

10  Ralph Buxton

10  Jess Flores

10  Bill Schuster

# MAJOR LEAGUE PLAYERS
# PRODUCED BY THE PCL
## (Partial/Unofficial)

Although some of the following players began in other circuits, I consider all to be products of the PCL.

| | | |
|---|---|---|
| Ken Aspromonte | Jess Flores | Andy Patko |
| Gene Baker | Jim Grant | Roy Partee |
| Ed Bailey | Art Houtteman | Albie Pearson |
| Earl Battey | Fred Hutchinson | Ray Prim |
| Gene Bearden | Larry Jansen | Bob Purkey |
| Marv Breeding | Jackie Jensen | Vic Raschi |
| Ernie Broglio | Nippy Jones | Rudy Regalado |
| Lew Burdette | Marty Keough | Floyd Robinson |
| Jim Busby | Johnny Lindell | Al Rosen |
| Jerry Casale | Ernie Lombardi | Art Schallock |
| Rocky Colavito | Dale Long | Harry Simpson |
| Billy Consolo | Peanuts Lowrey | Roy Smalley |
| Dom Dallesandro | Billy Martin | Dick Stuart |
| Dom DiMaggio | Bill Mazeroski | Willie Tasby |
| Walt Dropo | Cal McLish | Earl Torgeson |
| Ryne Duren | Orestis Minoso | Bill Werle |
| Luke Easter | Red Munger | Maury Wills |
| Don Elston | Ray Noblé | Gene Woodling |
| Ferris Fain | Irv Noren | Gus Zernial |

# ON THE WAY UP

The following thumbnail sketches will give you a little idea of how some players performed in the PCL before going to the majors. You will also see how they did upon reaching the big leagues. They will be listed in alphabetical but not chronological order.

### GENE BAKER — SHORTSTOP

Gene Baker came to the PCL in 1950 and had four solid years with the Los Angeles Angels. He hit .290, .278, .260 and .294, respectively. He went to the Chicago Cubs in 1954, where he shifted, to second base. Baker and the great Ernie Banks formed the first black double-play combination in the major leagues. They teamed up at the keystone for four and one-half years and collectively did a good job with the glove and bat. By the way, it was Ernie Banks who replaced Roy Smalley at shortstop for Chicago.

### GENE BEARDEN — PITCHER

Gene Bearden, a left-handed pitcher, had two strong years with Oakland in 1946 and 1947. He was 15 and 4 in 1946 and 16 and 7 in 1947. His ERA in 1947 was 2.86. He went up to the Cleveland Indians in 1948 and won 20 games, while losing only 7. His 2.43 ERA led the American League. He never had another winning year after that amazing rookie season. Bearden was nonetheless a fine pitcher and one I remember well in the PCL, both before and after his major league days.

### FERRIS FAIN — FIRST BASE

Ferns Fain came into the Coast League in 1939 with the San Francisco Seals at the age of 17. He played in only 12 games and hit .212. He became the regular first baseman for the Seals in 1940, but missed several years because of World War II. In 1941, he hit .319 and had a league-leading 122 runs scored. In 1946, he hit .301 and again led the league in runs scored, 117. That same year he had a league-leading 112 RBI's. He played with the Philadelphia Athletics, Chicago White Sox, and the Detroit Tigers. He won back-to-back batting titles in 1951 and 1952 while playing with the lowly A's.

### FRED HUTCHINSON — PITCHER

Fred Hutchinson was 18 years old when he broke in with his hometown team, the Seattle Rainiers, in 1938. He also appeared in the League before and after his major league days. He returned to the Coast League not as a player, but as a manager. He was nothing short of phenomenal in that rookie year of 1938, winning 25 and losing only 7 games. His ERA was 2.48. He pitched in 35 games and amassed 290 innings of work. From 1946 through 1951, he won 87 games with the Detroit Tigers. "Hutch" was known to be a fierce competitor.

### LARRY JANSEN — PITCHER

Larry Jansen pitched with San Francisco in 1941, '42, '45, and '46. The 1946 season saw him win 30 games and lose 6. His ERA was a super 1.57. He went to the New York Giants in 1947 and posted a 21–5 record. Larrv had a big in 1951, winning 23 games and doing more than his share in helping the Giants wipe out the Dodgers' 19-game lead and bring a National League pennant to New York.

### BILLY MARTIN — SECOND BASE

Billy Martin was born in Berkeley and played in neighboring Oakland part of the 1947 season and all of 1948 and 1949. The last two years he hit .277 and .286. He had a colorful playing career, especially with the New York Yankees, for whom he played eight seasons (1950–1957). He appeared in five World Series and averaged .333 with the bat. Little or no comment need be made concerning Billy as a manager. He remains colorful and indeed is fiery. I cannot agree with everything that he does, but I recognize him to be a most knowledgeable baseball man and one who expects his players not to make any mental errors, while expecting them to work hard so as to cut down on physical miscues.

Rich Timmis told me that Billy often would attend some semi-pro games in the Bay area when his season had concluded. He noticed some flaws in Rich's play and volunteered to help him sharpen up his skills on the infield. He worked with Rich several days and never let on who he was, although everyone knew. Yes, Billy is known for most every negative thing he does. But I'm glad to report this story, which clearly indicates that Billy Martin, just like you and me, has far more strong points than weak ones.

### ORESTIS MINOSO — INFIELD-OUTFIELD

Orestis "Minnie" Minoso was one of four black players I remember who came into the PCL in 1949. He was with San Diego in 1949 and 1950, hitting .297 and .339. In his second year he had 203 hits and 115 RBI's. He played with the Chicago White Sox from 1951 to 1957, and was always known as an extremely exciting and popular player. He is said to have put the "GO" in the Go-Go White Sox.

### BILL WERLE — PITCHER

Bill Werle was born in Oakland but began his Coast League career with San Francisco. Werle, a southpaw, pitched for the Seals from 1943 to 1948. He missed one year of PCL play because of the war. He was a very durable pitcher, pitching 175 innings or more from 1946 to 1948. He played in the majors with Pittsburgh and St. Louis, but arm trouble stopped him from reaching his potential.

# PLAYERS WHO FURTHERED
# THEIR CAREERS IN THE PCL
## (Partial/Unofficial)

Earl Averill, Sr.
Frank Baumholtz
Gene Bearden[1]
Floyd Bevens
Ewell Blackwell
Cy Blanton
Cy Block
Johnny Beradino
Tommy Byrne
Dolph Camilli[4]
Loyd Christopher
Rip Collins[4]
Babe Dahlgren
Dom Dallesandro[1]
Vince DiMaggio
Karl Drews
Jimmy Dykes[2]
Bob Elliott[4]
Nick Etten
Ferris Fain[1]

Jess Flores[1]
Augie Galan[4]
Charlie Gassaway
Joe Gordon[4]
Tom Hafey
Bucky Harris[2]
Spencer Harris
Clint Hartung
Babe Herman
Gene Hermanski
Rogers Hornsby[2]
Fred Hutchinson[3]
Monty Irvin
Eddie Joost[4]
Spider Jorgenson
Ken Keltner
Danny Kravitz
Cookie Lavagetto
Johnny Lindell[1]
Danny Litwhiler

Dano Lodigiani
Ernie Lombardi[1]
Pepper Martin[4]
George Metkovich[4]
Red Munger[1]
Lefty O'Doul[4]
Mel Ott[2]
Roy Partee[1]
Jerry Priddy[4]
Jimmy Reese[5]
Charlie Root[4]
Marius Russo
Luke Sewell[2]
Jigger Statz[4]
Bill Sweeney[4]
Eric Tipton
Lou Tost[1]
Johnny Van Der Meer
Dick Wakefield
Jo Jo White[4]

[1]Appeared in PCL before and after major league service.
[2]Appeared in the PCL as a manager.
[3]Appeared in PCL before the majors as a player, and after as a manager.
[4]Appeared in the PCL as a player and a manager.
[5]Player and Coach.

# MAJOR LEAGUE MANAGERS AND
# COACHES PRODUCED BY THE PCL
## (Partial/Unofficial)

Red Adams – Coach
Sparky Anderson – Manager
George Bamberger – Coach & Mgr.

Bobby Bragan – Manager
Jim Busby – Coach
Rocky Colavito – Coach

Monty Basgall – Coach
Cloyd Boyer – Coach
Herman Franks – Manager
Owen Friend – Coach
Marv Grissom – Coach
Roy Hartsfield – Manager
Al Heist – Coach
Fred Hutchinson – Manager
Clyde King – Manager & Coach
Hub Kittle – Coach
Tom Lasorda – Coach & Manager
Don Leppert – Coach
Peanuts Lowrey – Coach
Harry Malmberg – Coach
Billy Martin – Manager
Jim Marshall – Manager
Gene Mauch – Manager

Billy Consolo – Coach
Jim Fanning – Manager
Bill Mazeroski – Coach
Cal McLish – Coach
Charlie Metro – Coach & Manager
Don Osborn – Coach
Jack Paepke – Coach
Bill Rigney – Manager
Larry Shepherd – Manager & Coach
Larry Sherry – Coach
Mayo Smith – Manager
Elvin Tappe – Manager
Wayne Terwilliger – Coach
Lee Walls – Coach
Jo Jo White – Coach
Maury Wills – Manager

# PCL PLAYERS WHOSE SONS PLAYED PROFESSIONAL BASEBALL
## (Partial/Unofficial)

| Father | Son |
|---|---|
| Earl Averill, Sr. | Earl Averill, Jr. |
| Gus Bell | Buddy Bell |
| Ray Boone | Bob Boone |
| Dolph Camilli | Doug Camilli |
| Len Gabrielsen, Sr. | Len Gabrielsen, Jr. |
| Marty Keough | Matt Keough |
| Ron Northey | Scott Northey |
| Jack Paepke | Dennis Paepke |
| Paul Pettit | Mark Pettit/Timothy Pettit |
| Herm Pillette | Duane Pillette |
| Mel Queen, Sr. | Mel Queen, Jr. |
| Hal Rhyne, Sr. | Hal Rhyne, Jr. |
| Leo Righetti | Dave Righetti |
| Earl Sheely | Hollis "Bud" Sheely |
| Roy Smalley, Jr. | Roy Smalley III |

| Mike Tresh | Tom Tresh |
| Al Unser | Del Unser |
| Jo Jo White | Mike White |
| Maury Wills | Elliott "Bump" Wills |

# THE BLACK PLAYER
# IN THE PCL

The inequities and injustices of the black man were evident in professional sports during most of my PCL days. In looking back, I find it hard to believe that I can remember when there were no black players allowed in professional baseball. The first two I remember in the PCL were **Booker T. McDaniels** and **Artie Wilson**. Both came into the League in 1949, just a few short years after Jackie Robinson had broken the color line in the major leagues.*

**BOOKER T. McDANIELS**, a pitcher, was the very first black player I recall, being signed by the Los Angeles Angels. He appeared in 18 games, completing half of his starts. His record was eight victories and nine defeats. He struck out 60 batters and gave up 59 walks. His earned-run average was 4.22. He played with the Angels again in 1950 and appeared in 37 games, with a record of three wins and four losses. His ERA was 6.49.

**ARTIE WILSON** was the next I remember, coming to the Coast League from the Negro American League. Wilson literally came in with a bang, and how sweet it must have been. San Diego signed him first and he appeared in 31 games for the Padres before moving on to Oakland, where he played in 134 games. All Wilson did was lead the League in hitting, with a lofty .348 batting average. He had 211 hits, 248 total bases, walked 62 times and stole 47 bases. Wilson was an infielder and he played with five PCL teams: San Diego, Oakland, Seattle, Portland and Sacramento. He batted left and threw right.

---

*For the record, I believe **John Ritchey** was the first black player to appear in the PCL (1948 – San Diego).

# BLACK PLAYERS REMEMBERED
## (Partial/Unofficial)

| | | |
|---|---|---|
| Frankie Austin | Marshall Bridges | Luke Easter |
| Gene Baker | Bill Causion | Jim Grant |
| Earl Battey | Benny Daniels | Lenny Green |
| Charlie Beamon | Lino Donoso | Jehosie Heard |
| Bob Boyd | Solly Drake | Monty Irvin |
| Booker T. McDaniels | Curt Roberts | Willie Tasby |
| Orestis Minoso | Floyd Robinson | Joe Taylor |
| Ray Noblé | Harry Simpson | Bob Thurman |
| Dave Pope | Milt Smith | Roy Welmaker |
| George Prescott | Theolic Smith | Maury Wills |
| John Ritchey | R. C. Stevens | Artie Wilson |

Of this list, I believe Luke Easter, Monty Irvin, Orestis Minoso and Maury Wills were the most successful in the major leagues. Of these four, Wills was No. 1. I remember seeing him play with Seattle in 1957 and thought him to be one who would never go too far. He certainly proved me to be wrong.

There was a good reason for this: namely, that he was a quick learner. As a hitter, Wills was an average right-handed batter at best. Bobby Bragan successfully made him a switch hitter when they were together at Spokane. Wills became a genius at pounding the ball into the skin surface of the infield for base hits, especially when batting left-handed. He also became adept at lining well-placed shots over the infielders' heads. Further, he succeeded because of his base stealing ability, which is a matter for discussion yet today. I personally never thought Maury to be super fast, but he came to know every pitcher's weakness when it came to holding on runners. This, along with his own strengths, made him a base-stealing terror for years.

I have been dismayed many times over the years when I observed athletes who settled far short of their potential. Wills totally rejected this idea. I'm convinced my initial feelings about him would have been correct had it not been for his sheer determination to awaken and then use every positive mental and physical tool at his disposal.

# THE SWITCH HITTERS
## (Partial/Unofficial)

From the list of switch hitters that will follow, over half are pitchers. This means that these hurlers who swung the bat from both sides should more appropriately be called "switch batters."

Cecil Garriott of Los Angeles was the first switch hitter that I remember. The year was 1944, which just happened to be his best in the Coast League. He hit .286 and had 13 home runs. I remember Garriott as being a better left-handed hitter, and if I recall correctly, he hit only from the left side in 1947 and 1950. He did return to switch hitting in 1951, where he appeared in only six games.

The only other switch hitter I feel qualified to discuss was Albie Glossop, a utility infielder also of the Los Angeles Angels. He played several years with the Angels and had a big year in 1948. He hit .283 with 17 home runs. It is my opinion that Glossop performed better as a part-time player. He seemed to struggle when playing on a regular basis. I consider him to be the most successful pinch hitter of anyone I recall in the Coast League. He, like Garriott, was a better left-handed batter.

| | | |
|---|---|---|
| Gene Bearden* | Charlie Gassaway* | Leon Mohr |
| Stanislaus Breard | Albie Glossop | Art Pennington |
| Marshall Bridges* | Joe Gonzales* | Tony Ponce* |
| Italo Chelini* | Clarence Hicks | Jean Roy* |
| Bob Chesnes* | Ed Ignasiak | James Russell |
| Syd Cohen* | Clarence Iott* | Ed St. Claire |
| Gene Corbett | Don Kaiser | Mike Sandlock |
| Solly Drake | Chris Kitsos | Tom Seats* |
| Charles Eisenmann* | Doyle Lade* | Bill Seinsoth* |
| Glenn Elliott* | Al Lein* | Edgar Smith* |
| Ed Fernandes | Garth Mann* | Theolic Smith* |
| Charles Fischer* | Herschel Martin | William Wietelman |
| Augie Galan | Cal McLish* | Casey Wise |
| Cecil Garriott | Russ Meyer* | Del Young |

*Pitcher

predominantly right-handed pitchers. Yeah, you're right—every one of those four were natural right-handed batters.

I had the opportunity of converting my first baseman, Dan Ross, into a switch hitter and he became a better left-handed batter. This boy was with me all four years and he was a super kid. He didn't give me one minute of trouble. This was really saying something, since the hair of everyone whoever managed in the Little League either turns gray or turns loose.

# THE BATTING ORDER

The batting order in the PCL had two established constants. They never changed during all the years I followed the Coast League. One was as it should be; namely, that the pitcher hit in the ninth spot. The other was as it not necessarily should be; namely, that the catcher always batted eighth. Only in reflection did I realize how wrong this really was, although at the time I thought that was the way it should be. I talked with my friend and former neighbor, Herb McFarland, about this subject, as he is far more into baseball research than I. He was raised in Pittsburgh and was close to all major league happenings. He informed me that this procedure was a part of big league baseball in yesteryear. The real break came in 1929, when there was no way to keep the slugging Mickey Cochrane so low in the order.

Herb did point out that some catchers did bat in the seventh spot, but the overwhelming number in both leagues from 1903 to 1928 hit eighth. After Cochrane came the likes of Bill Dickey, and a short time later, Walker Cooper. After them came two great hitting catchers, Roy Campanella and Yogi Berra. These receivers all hit in the power spots. More recently, catchers Thurman Munson and Johnny Bench hit in the three, four or five position.

What simply happened was that the major leagues properly moved away from the accepted procedure of locking their catchers in the number eight spot, while the PCL, at least in my time, did not. I'm not suggesting that every PCL catcher did not belong in the eighth position. I am saying that many deserved to hit higher up.

While on the subject of catchers, it should be pointed out that another constant existed in the PCL. No catcher, barring injury, ever caught both ends of a double header. The regular catcher caught the first game, while the backup catcher caught the second. Jim Gladd may have been an exception. He caught 30 consecutive games for Hollywood in 1948. It is very probable, though, that no double headers were scheduled during his streak.

## DOUBLE HEADERS AND IRON MEN

Double headers were certainly a regular part of PCL baseball in my day. One feature that was different in the minor leagues then, and, still is today, is the fact that they play only seven innings in the second game. So used to this procedure was I that I thought it odd the first time I heard that major league teams played nine innings in the second game of a twin bill.

I can recall that PCL double headers were now and then used for certain pitchers to attempt the "iron man feat" of pitching both games. I remember Tony Ponce of San Francisco did it against the Angels on the last day of the 1953 season. He won both games, 4 to 2 in game one and 1 to 0 in game two.

Well, we've long since seen the last of this kind of stunt. With all the million-dollar arms around today and the ever-increasing number of rotator cuff candidates, this is surely a no-no in baseball today, and it should be. Nowadays pitchers are carefully watched, and I doubt there are very many, if any, overworked hurlers.

One reason is that most teams use a five-man rotation. If there be an exception, it would be as regards American League hurlers. Junior circuit pitchers simply stay in games longer because of the Designated Hitter Rule. I admit this controversial regulation will doubtless take its toll on pitchers in both years and velocity.

# THE PLAYING
# SURFACES

For those who have seen games in all or most of the old PCL parks, can any of you recall the playing surfaces as being a topic of major concern? I can't. This subject is, to me, most fascinating, and is especially controversial at the major league level right up to the present time.

In my time the skin part of every PCL infield was composed of nothing but dirt (profound statement). Now, it would go without saying that some of these surfaces had to be better than others, but my memory fails to record there being much to-do about playing surfaces in those days.

Can that be said in these times of sophistication? I think not. We've seen a lot of crushed brick, and would you believe one major league infield is purported to be a mixture of crushed brick and lava. I refer to this as a favorite recipe of some gourmet groundskeeper. Some have reported this surface as being the worst in the major leagues. At any rate, we constantly hear and read nowadays of much unhappiness concerning infields. The point in this discourse being that not all modern ideas are always for the better.*

While on this subject, I would also say that the grass in PCL parks appeared to be uniform in height, and the tampering of the infield near the baseline (degrees of slope) was nonexistent. Maybe I was too naive and therefore unaware of subtle skulduggery. But I don't think so.

Lest you get the idea that I believe everything in the past was better, we all know that many features have been added to make the game safer. One such advantageous change was the warning track. There were none in the PCL. Further, most fences are padded or protected in major league parks today. No such safety devices were in evidence in the PCL in my time.

---

*The Angels always dragged their infield by using manpower. Hollywood used motor power, a red Cushman motor scooter. The Stars for many years touched up their infield at the end of the fifth inning. One Hollywood announcer referred to this procedure as the "facial fifth."

Even without modern innovations I would give every old PCL park that I've been in a passing grade with respect to playing surfaces.

# SPRING TRAINING

What could one possibly say about Spring Training in the PCL? In my case, virtually nothing if it weren't for the fact that Oscar Vitt brought his 1941 Portland Beavers here to my hometown of Santa Monica for Spring Training. This was big news and we did have a stadium, Municipal Stadium. It was in all respects a disaster.

From my early childhood I have only the memory of how tired that structure really was. At any rate, here came the likes of Herm Reich, Marvin Owen, Johnny Gill, Frankie Hawkins, Ted Norbert, Ad Liska and Byron Speece. Of course the team was quartered at the lavish Carmel Hotel, which was Santa Monica's most elegant inn at the time. Although old Municipal Stadium is long gone, the Carmel Hotel remains. It is now pretty much of an old folks' home. Come to think of it, it was pretty much of an old folks' home back in 1941.

Getting back to Municipal Stadium, there really was plenty of playing space. In addition to the main stadium playing field, there were three good-sized softball diamonds on the site. I remember how excited I was to play on those fields with older men in the City League, being a junior in high school when I started.

In all seriousness, I remember our city doing its best to make the Portland team welcome and happy during their stay in our town. Our local newspaper, the *Evening Outlook*, gave excellent coverage concerning everything the team did; I still remember the large picture of Oscar Vitt which appeared in our paper the day the team arrived. He was beaming from ear to ear. He was still smiling when the team broke camp to start the season.

He was, however, not smiling at the conclusion of the 1941 PCL season, I don't know if training at old Municipal Stadium gave Portland a defeatist complex or not. I do know they ended up in last place that year. They won 71 games and lost 97 and were 33 games behind the champion Seattle Rainiers. I can tell you that the Portland team did not return to Santa Monica in 1942, and Oscar Vitt did not return as manager of the team. I can also tell you that Portland finished the 1942 season once again in the cellar, winning 67 and losing 110. The change of spring training sites didn't help the hapless Beavers and their new manager, Frank Brazill.*

The only other time I ever saw a Spring Training game was in 1956. My friend Dave Barton, now an eminent surgeon, and I went to Palm Springs in the hopes of seeing Paul Pettit play. He was not, however, in the lineup that day.

In the 1950s some, but not all, Hollywood training games were broadcast on radio. I always listened to those games.

### SPRING TRAINING

*It's been a cold, cold winter, but when snow begins to melt,*
*I get that certain something that for many years I've felt.*

*It's a joyous, happy feeling that bubbles in my heart.*
*It means we'll soon have baseball; Spring Training's 'bout to start.*

*There'll be many raw-boned rookies with peach fuzz on each face*
*Eagerly awaiting the starting of the race.*

*We'll see the seasoned graybeard who has no doubt or fear*
*That he can do the job required, at least for one more year.*

*At close of camp they're weary, but disappointment? Not a trace.*
*For every player knows his team will end up in first place!*

*KS*

---

*The war years brought about a change in the way Spring Training was usually conducted. By 1943 it was difficult, even impossible, for many PCL teams to train at the sites of their choice. Some squads were forced to find a location closer to home; others trained at their home parks. It is true that some players even trained at their own homes.

Spring Training 1949, Sacramento vs. Folsom Prison Inmates.

# THE CHEERLEADER

It is commonplace in present-day baseball to see many interesting individuals who, though only fans, are more than conspicuous by their very presence, dress and actions. Here in my part of the country, a Tarzan-like character is often seen and heard at Dodger Stadium. Several "out-front" self-proclaimed cheerleaders have also surfaced at Anaheim Stadium. These were considerably more conservative in dress and demeanor and never remained on the scene too long. By way of television, we've seen the large bearded man in Baltimore who stands on the roof of the Oriole dugout and leads the fans in his animated Oriole spell-out. Also by way of the tube, we have seen the ever-increasing number of fancy dressed animal characters who entertain and stir up the fans.

In my days of watching baseball in the PCL all of the above types of individuals were nonexistent. I do, however, want to tell you of one fan who stands out in my mind as a cheerleader in her favorite stadium. It should be understood that she in no way fits the description of the type of cheerleaders we see today, be they animal characters or just plain fans.

She was known as **Angel Annie**, and as you might suspect, her team was the Los Angeles Angels. I don't really remember how long she was around. I recall hearing and seeing her in the early 1950s. Her claim to fame was her ability and willingness to utter a shrill, one-note sound at various times during a game. Knowledgeable musicians would probably agree that it was at least one octave above middle C. As to the length of this sound, it never occurred to me to time it. Let's just say it was from two to three seconds long. Even though I heard her many times through the radio, I only saw her once. By accident, I was seated five or six rows from her one night at Wrigley Field. The stands were not too crowded and I could easily observe her. I judged her to be in her 60's. She wore an Angel cap and was bundled up in a blanket and sat alone. To observe her was to love her, and everyone did.

My conclusion about this wonderful lady was that even though her sound was penetrating, she didn't have the slightest

thought of calling attention to herself. This was simply her way of telling the team that she cared about them. She remained seated throughout the entire game and rarely changed facial expression. She seemed to be in no way embarrassed or to care what anyone thought of her.

What a great gal, this Angel Annie!

## THE GRANDSTAND MANAGER

Since the incidents I am about to relate took place at Gilmore Field, I rightfully should have placed this subject in the earlier section specifically dealing with the Hollywood Stars. I elected to put it here in the league section, since this subject is so overwhelmingly inclusive of every PCL stadium or any other baseball stadium for that matter.

If you and I are really honest, we'll admit that we've all done our share of "managing" from our seats in the stands. Now, most of us relate our feelings in semi-docile tones to the ones sitting next to us by pointing out something like, "Why is manager so-

and-so playing 'All Thumbs Theodore' at third, when he should be playing 'Sweet Glove Gus' there!" We have often raised the decibels by calling "Forlorn Freddie" a bum for striking out, even though he had two hits in his previous trips to the plate. His striking out clearly indicated to everyone that he never should have been in the lineup in the first place. We knew it, why didn't the manager? Well, there are some "managers" that make you and me look like gentle kittens by comparison. These highly vocal, would-be field generals were at their best when some of us would be their audience.

You can be sure that whenever I was close enough to one of these individuals I wasn't about to miss his fervent comments. After all, I still had two good eyes to view the action, why not lend an ear to one who without doubt could have been baseball's greatest manager?

I remember being in attendance at a game between Hollywood and Sacramento in 1947 when a grandstand manager surfaced in the row in back of me. This guy really had it in for

Sacramento skipper Dick Bartell. It was necessary for Bartell to trek toward the mound several times to make pitching changes. Of those he brought in, not one satisfied this guy. The pitchers were less than bush and Bartell was a blundering ignoramus for having brought them in. Bartell, in this fellow's opinion, was also most inept in his use of pinch hitters, being somewhere between a pea-brained ninny and a babbling simpleton when it came to selecting the right pinch hitters to bring Sacramento back from sure defeat.

You can imagine that with Hollywood out in front I was feeling happy about the proceedings. This being the case, I acted as if I agreed with our friend in his evaluation of Bartell, hoping he'd continue his tirade, which he did. Not only did he continue to remind us of his dislike for Bartell, but he told Bartell himself several times by loud vocal outbursts leveled at the manager when he came onto the field. This he did in words and tone not befitting a bedtime story.

Well, it all came to an end with Hollywood winning, Bartell surviving, my still having two good eyes, but only one good ear. Situations like this were repeated numerous times and I most fondly remember them.

# EXPERT JUDGES
# OF TALENT

Still tied into the subject of grandstand managers, there are those who could more accurately be called "experts" on the subject of player personnel. The only problem with these people, as was the case with the other type of grandstand manager, is that they had nothing good or constructive to say.

I remember one night in the late 1940s, a Hollywood out-fielder whose name I could give misplayed a base hit into extra bases and I immediately caught the wrath of one of these "experts." After listening to this guy for several innings, I frankly admit I, too, had serious doubts as to why this ball player was even in uniform, much less in the game. I can't say that what happened that night occurred very often, but this guy succeeded in rallying a rather large number of fans in collectively staying on the outfielder right up to the game's conclusion. This they did in a seemingly endless chorus of boos and uncomplimentary expressions which clearly illustrated the total uselessness of this oufielder in the home white uniform.

I remember my reactions were totally different than they were in the other incident. I felt extremely sorry for this player. Even though we never did, my buddy Tracy and I talked about writing him a letter to cheer him up.

One thing is certain, and that is that the time will never come when we won't have these grandstand managers, nor can any player who has ever put on a pair of cleats hope to escape for too long the verbal blasts and downright abuse of these "expert judges of talent."

### "THE MANAGER"

*Each team they have a boss man, da manager be his name.*
*He make da big decision when they play da ol' ballgame.*
*He prepare a startin' lineup tellin' da boys jist where to play*
*So they go about their bizness simple doin' os he say.*

*Sometime he look real super and da game it go'd real good.*
*He had no worry 'bout it; he knowed it shorly would.*
*But they times when he be stupid, like bringin' Nicely up ta hit,*
*When "Bruggie" Ogrodowski'd do a better job of it.*

*One boss he brung Roy Helser ta pitch ta Jo Jo White;*
*He simple hit da first pitch far out into da nite.*
*If he'd brung Ad Liska, Jo Jo would no git a hit.*
*He'd strike him out a-swingin'.*
*Da ball be found in Younker' mitt.*

*Why they not ask me ta be boss man, I jist cain't understand.*
*I still tell 'em how ta do it from atop da ol' grandstand.*

*KS*

# WHAT DID THEY DO AFTER BASEBALL?

If I had my way, I'd prepare and present a list containing the names of every former Coast League player indicating what he did, or is doing, by way of employment. This is totally impossible, since I personally have heard so little in this regard. If available, the list of successful ex-ballplayers would number into the hundreds, since the only criteria for success in my book are that one does his best in his chosen profession and that he achieves peace of mind in the doing.

Having said this, there are those who have attained lofty positions both in and out of the game after they hung up their cleats. Since we do hear about some of these people, and since what they have chosen to do is interesting and worthy of comment, let's mention a few names under the following headings:

### The ACTORS
### The SONGWRITER
### The BROADCASTERS
### The BASEBALL EXECUTIVES
### The COLLEGE EXECUTIVES

# THE ACTORS

Many remember **Chuck Connors**, former Los Angeles first baseman who starred in the 1950s television series *The Rifleman*. This was a very successful show and brought the former Angel first sacker far more fame and fortune than he ever attained while playing baseball.

My records show that Connors played no more than two seasons in the Coast League. In 1951 he hit .321 in 98 games, which impressed the parent Chicago Cubs enough to call him up during the season, dispatching Cub first baseman Dee Fondy to take his place. Fondy hit .376 with the Angels with 11 home runs in 70 games. The 1952 season saw Fondy back up and Connors

back down. This, I assume, had a hand in his turning to something else. Connors has made numerous television and movie appearances. He operates a ranch in California.

**Johnny Beradino** is another ex-Coast Leaguer who is now famous as a result of his turning to acting. He is the mythical Dr. Steve Hardy in the daytime soap opera *General Hospital*. If you want any information on him as an actor, I can't help you since I have become addicted only to coffee, not soap operas. As the youth have been known to say, "This is not my bag." I can assure you of one thing, though. Beradino has weathered many a crisis and escaped from countless desperate situations while in front of the camera. At this writing, he's still hanging in there, doubtless ministering to human need with the utmost of compassion.

Beradino was an infielder and played in the PCL in 1950 with both San Diego and Sacramento. He played in the majors with several teams, which included the Boston Red Sox, Detroit Tigers and the St. Louis Browns.

**Bill Schuster** and **George Metkovich** are two of many former PCL players who have appeared in baseball movies. Schuster appeared in the story of Grover Cleveland Alexander, which starred Ronald Reagan. He also appeared in *The Pride of the Yankees*. These men were used in pictures because of their baseball ability and did not act professionally in movies to my knowledge after their playing days were over.

# THE SONGWRITER

When you hear the name **Harry Ruby**, does it bring back memories of one who set the Coast League ablaze with his hot bat? I think not. Since Harry Ruby did indeed "play" in the PCL and since our informal talk by design involves a variety of subjects surrounding former PCL players both on and off the field, I want to tell you of this man.

Harry Ruby was the music writer from the musical team of Bert Kalmar and Harry Ruby. This tandem produced songs which made them musical comedy's greatest team of the 1920s. Together they wrote such songs as *Thinking of You, Nevertheless, Who's Sorry Now, I Love You So Much,* and *Three Little Words*, title song of the MGM musical which came out in 1950 and starred Fred Astaire and Red Skelton.

If you know anything about Ruby, you must know that this man was a baseball fan through and through. Because of his popularity as a songwriter, he was often allowed to "horse around" with baseball clubs, particularly during spring training. I don't think I'm wrong when I say if this boy had been good enough he would have pursued a career in baseball, so intense was his love for the game. Insofar as his playing in the PCL is concerned, it could only be construed as a joke or kind gesture on someone's part. He was with the 1940 Los Angeles Angels and appeared in one game with no at bats, giving him a perfect .000 percentage.

I wouldn't be at all surprised if being in this one game meant as much, if not more, to him as writing his most famous song.

# THE BROADCASTERS

Of the former PCL players who moved from the field to the booth, I perhaps chief among those who gained national exposure was former Sacramento infielder **Robert "Bud" Blattner**. Blattner, as most of us know, was sidekick and straight man for the late Dizzy Dean when these two did the *Game of the Week* on network television. I, more often than not, felt sorry for Bud, since he was many times maneuvered into admitting how poor a hitter and infielder he was, while at the same time joining the rest of us listening to old Diz extol his many virtues and achievements out there on the hill. It is a fact, however, that somewhere in between Diz's rendition of "Wabash Cannonball," comments like *"He slud into third," "The runners got back to their respectable bases," "I suppose you seen that on your camree,"* along with some other occasional mention of the game in progress, Blattner did get some remarks in.

Yeah, I'm being a little facetious, but I want to describe a recording that Hollywood announcer Mark Scott played on a pre-game show one evening that bears me out in evaluating old Diz. The record began and ended with small talk, laughter, singing and stories. At no time was any comment made about the game that was in progress.

Whoever wrote the script beautifully kept the listener abreast of the game by using the public address announcer to let us know what was going on. In between the hilarity in the booth, in the background home runs were being hit and fantastic plays were being made. The idea that came across was that there was some super game going on which was worthy of description, but old Diz had other things on his mind.

I don't recall Bud having much to say, but he did get in an occasional "yeah" from time to time. I roared with laughter and find myself chuckling inside even now as I tell you about it. I cornered Mark Scott one night at Hollywood to see if there was some way to get a copy of that recording. He didn't know who at the studio had it, and I never heard it played again. Whether what I have just described was repeated in actuality too often for Bud I don't know, but he did eventually depart the old right hander.

Well, was Blattner really poor as a player, and what became of him as an announcer? Frankly, as a boy or a man, I have not been too much into statistics, although I see the need and importance of some of them. This being the case, I never realized until recent study that Bud Blattner had absolutely nothing to be ashamed of in his two years of play in the PCL. A partial list of his stats proves this:

| YEAR | AB | HITS | HR | RBI | AVERAGE |
|------|-----|------|-----|------|---------|
| 1940 | 442 | 123 | 4 | 54 | .278 |
| 1941 | 620 | 182 | 17 | 100 | .294 |

These stats were good enough to earn him a call to the majors in 1942.

As an announcer, I remember Blattner here on the West Coast as the voice of the Los Angeles/California Angels from 1962 to 1968. I then remember him as the voice of the Kansas City Royals, the only major league team I have had any serious involvement with since the realignment of the Coast League in 1958. But this is another story.

It is my understanding that Blattner is no longer in broadcasting. I believe he lives in the Lake of the Ozarks, Missouri.*

## ROY AND KING

Two other Coast Leaguers who I remember as being active as broadcasters are **Jean Pierre Roy** of Montreal, and **Nelson "Nellie" King** of the Pittsburgh Pirates. I can only offer supposition as to their qualifications for being behind the mike.

Roy is a French Canadian who speaks French and is obviously knowledgeable of the game. Montreal, of course, broadcasts their games in both French and English. Roy was a right-handed pitcher who first surfaced in the PCL with Sacramento in the early 1940s. I remember him later as a member of the Hollywood Stars, for whom he played in 1949 and 1950.

Nelson King is a tall, slim man and was also a right-handed pitcher who played with Hollywood. I remember him as being only with the Stars in 1955, where he had a record of two wins and three losses. His ERA was 3.70.

*Blattner had two words that he used quite often. One was "puppies," meaning feet; the other, "pumping," which referred to players running the bases.

I never met King, but saw him several times away from the stadium while following the team on the road. My impression of him was that he was quiet and reserved, which would seem to indicate his not being suited for broadcasting. I was certainly incorrect about that. His length of stay as an announcer with the Pirates clearly indicates that he must have been a good one.

# THE BASEBALL EXECUTIVES

The following is a partial list of former PCL players who held, or are currently holding, front office positions in baseball:

AL ROSEN – General Manager, Houston Astros

JIM BAUMER – General Manager, Milwaukee Brewers

BOBBY BRAGAN – President, Texas League
            Head of Speakers' Bureau, Texas Rangers

JOE BUZAS – Former General Manager in the minor leagues, and
            owner of no less than 48 baseball franchises in 13 cities

JIM FANNING – Front office executive, Montreal Expos

HERMAN FRANKS – General Manager, Chicago Cubs

EDDIE MULLIGAN – Part owner of several minor league baseball
            teams; President, California Baseball League

JACK PAEPKE – California Angels Speakers' Bureau

LES POWERS – Secretary/Business Manager, Hollywood Stars

DEWEY SORIANO – General Manager, Seattle Rainiers
            President PC1 1960–68
            Part owner of Seattle Pilots

HAYWOOD SULLIVAN – Part owner, Boston Red Sox

EDO VANNI – Traveling secretary, Seattle Rainiers

BEN WADE – Front office, Los Angeles Dodgers

GORDON GOLDSBERRY – Head of Chicago Cubs' Scouting Department

TUCK STAINBACK – Front office, Los Angeles Dodgers.

Please allow me to make a comment concerning this list of baseball executives, including the three broadcasters previously mentioned. Maybe you do not have the same reaction as me, but think about it. With all due respect to superstars, baseball has never made superstardom a prerequisite for leadership among qualified former players who want to remain in the game in some capacity at the end of their playing days. Not only has baseball not suffered because of that fact, but it has been so much the better because of it.

Re-examine the aforementioned names. I don't believe you'll find a superstar among them. Yet to me they are giants in this game of baseball. What about former PCL players George "Sparky" Anderson and Tom Lasorda, who didn't find the going all that easy in the League? (Lasorda did have some good seasons with the Dodgers' farm team at Montreal.) Their achievements as field leaders are a matter of record.

I pause to thank those in the game who are responsible for being perceptive and discerning of the talents of these men and many others, and then doing something about it.

## THE COLLEGE EXECUTIVES

Former San Diego pitcher **Al Olsen** and ex-Oakland outfielder **Jess Hill** made their marks as athletic directors at two California universities—Olsen at San Diego State and Hill at the University of Southern California. Hill played football at USC and was the head coach there before becoming Athletic Director.

## FROM FOOTBALL
## TO BASEBALL

**Jackie Jensen**, former California Bear All-American running back, and **Eric Tipton**, who starred with the Duke Blue Devils, were two greats of the gridiron who left the pigskin for the horsehide.

Jensen played in the outfield for Oakland on his way to an out-standing career in the major leagues with the New York Yankees, Boston Red Sox and Washington Senators. He led the AL three times in RBI's and was the League MVP in 1958. Jensen's aversion to flying cut short what was a very successful major league career.

Tipton, unlike Jensen, came to the PCL at the close of his major league days. He played with Portland for one season only, 1952, having previously performed in the majors with the Phillies and Reds.

I never think of Eric Tipton but what memories of the 1939 Rose Bowl Game between USC and Duke come to mind. Now, I realize if I'm going to be absolutely true to the theme of these writings, you'd expect that a story is coming up of utmost interest surrounding Tipton as a player with Portland—but not so. Perhaps if I say this upcoming story recounts an embarrassing

moment in the life of former Portland Beaver outfielder Eric Tipton, you'll let me go ahead.

Tracy Jones is an old buddy of mine who attended many a PCL game with me. In addition to his interest in baseball, he loved college football, being an avid UCLA supporter. He and his older brother maintained a pictorial record of Rose Bowl games dating far back. Thanks to them, I can pass on a story that one Eric Tipton might wish forgotten (not really).

The season was 1938 and it was a most memorable one for Duke University. Not only did their football team go undefeated, but they went the entire season without being scored on. Because of this great achievement, Duke was invited to meet USC in the January 1, 1939 Rose Bowl Game. As a nine-year-old boy, I will never forget that game. It would have to be among the top Rose Bowl nail-biters. Its finish was indeed storybook. What I didn't know until sometime around 1947 or 1948 was that Tipton and another Duke player were so certain their team would defeat the Trojans, they made a most unusual vow. They declared that if Duke lost that game they would wear a pair of women's panties from Pasadena back home to Durham, North Carolina.

Had they only declared it, maybe they could have later denied having said it, but unfortunately they allowed a picture to be taken showing both of them holding onto a corner of the object of their vow. I can still see that picture from Tracy's Rose Bowl album. Well, it looked like Tipton and his friend had nothing to worry about as Duke got into the waning seconds of that game, hanging onto a three-to-nothing lead. The precious seconds were ticking off the clock and all hope seemed lost for Troy, when they suddenly connected for a game-winning touchdown pass which brought about a change in the style of underwear Tipton and his buddy would be wearing for the next few days. Final score: USC 7, Duke 3.

Over forty years have gone by, and I've often wondered if those two were true to their vow. I wrote to Mr. Tipton to see if he'd give me the true word about this. I'm happy to report that he did respond to my letter. He sent along a football picture from his days at Duke University and a warm letter. This man has literally spent a lifetime in sports. Portions of his letter reveal:

> Fourteen years in professional baseball;
> Coaching in both baseball and football at William and Mary
>    in the off season until 1957;
> Twenty years of coaching baseball and football at the United States
>    Military Academy, after which he retired.

He indicated that he and his teammates at Duke have mantained contact across the years. Upon receipt of my letter, he had just returned from the forty-third reunion of the January 1, 1939, Rose Bowl Game (1938 season). They first got together every ten years, then every five years. They now meet once a year.

Now, about the vow. Here is Eric's quote from his letter:

> As for the panties, I would have carried out that "vow," but
> I couldn't get them on—*too small*. (Ha!)

I'm glad I decided to write this man. When I first contacted him, I mentioned that he had to be a most interesting person— he is truly that. I appreciate his adding to these writings by filling us in on this celebrated "vow."

# FAVORITE AND MOST

Under this heading, I will be telling you of my personal PCL favorites. I hope by now that in some measure what I have written has brought many stories and incidents to the minds of you old-timers. As I tell you of my favorites, allow yourself the excitement of thinking of yours. This will make our nostalgic journey more fun.

# FAVORITE PCL PLAYER

What constitutes a great hitter? It is the ability to hit for average, hit with power, and drive in runs. My favorite player possessed all of these qualities. I vividly remember his batting stance, where he held the bat low (he used a 35-oz. bat). He was in every sense a pure hitter. No pitcher could ever get him out consistently. In the power department, hitting 20 or more home runs per season was not unusual for him. He hit over 170 in the PCL. His best power year was 1950, when he hit 39 homers at Portland. In eleven seasons, he hit under .300 only twice (not including 1946, when he appeared in only nine games). His best RBI year was 1951 when he knocked in 133 runs, also at Portland. My unofficial records have him with 823 RBI's. If he had any weakness, it was not at the plate. He could do it all with the bat! And in addition to his prowess there, he was a good outfielder, with an excellent arm. He stands 6' 3" and his playing weight was 195.

Anxious to get a picture and autograph of my favorite player, I wrote him and requested same. Not only did he comply, but took time to phone me and thank me for my interest in him. Can you imagine my surprise and joy? I will never forget it. What that phone call proved was that this man is a super human being. Now I will remember him not only as a great player, but as a great man.

My wife and I were privileged to be in his home in the summer of 1981. Believe me, we spent the entire evening talking nothing but baseball and looking over his memorabilia. He has a copy of a bat that bears his name. It felt like it weighed a ton when I tried to hold it up and assume a batting stance. He mentioned he had donated several personal baseball items to the Italian Hall of Fame, of which he is a member.

This man played with four Pacific Coast League teams: San Francisco, Portland, Sacramento and Oakland. My last opportunity to see him play was denied me in 1955. On my trip to Oakland that I mentioned earlier, I had high hopes of seeing him play. I missed him by approximately one week. The Cincinnati Reds purchased his contract and brought him up to be used as a pinch hitter. He was 33 years old at the time. The biggest mystery to me is how this man escaped being called up to the big leagues years earlier. Maybe I'm prejudiced, but I know he would have been successful in the majors. He retired at the close of the 1957 season.

His name is **Joe Brovia**.

"Joe Brovia was in a class by himself. He was one of the top three hitters I've seen in the League."

**ROGER BOWMAN**

"Joe Brovia was fearless and would not give one inch of ground to the pitcher in moving back or away from the plate."

**EDDIE BASINSKI**

# FAVORITE PCL COACH

**Jimmy Reese** is the premier coach in the Pacific Coast League. He also was a player, having played with both San Diego and Los Angeles. The former roommate of Babe Ruth was for many years a fixture on the coaching lines for the San Diego Padres, having served under many Padre managers.

Perhaps no field leader has ever been as highly thought of as this man, managers included. Many fans remember him for his fungo hitting. Though up in years, Reese is still active as a coach with the California Angels and still active with his fungo bat. I recently read where Angel players and officials presented him with a new car as a token of their love for him. Jimmy Reese totaled 40 years in the PCL as a player and a coach.

# FAVORITE PCL MANAGER

When it comes to managerial longevity in the PCL, no manager can match the great two-time National League batting champion **Frank J. (Lefty) O'Doul**. Not only did he manage in the League all twenty years of which I write, but he was a player as well.

His longest term as a manager with one team was spent with the San Francisco Seals. He managed there at least 14 years (I have no information prior to 1938). He managed three years at San Diego and then had the unusual distinction of managing four different PCL teams in four consecutive years—the afore-mentioned San Diego in 1954, Oakland in 1955, Vancouver in 1956, and Seattle in 1957. This consecutive streak, coupled with the 14 seasons he managed at San Francisco, meant that O'Doul piloted more PCL clubs from 1938 to 1957 than any other manager. (Bill Sweeney managed four teams.)

In the twenty years that Lefty managed, two of his teams finished in first place, four finished second, and one, third. O'Doul was certainly one of the most respected figures in the annals of the Pacific Coast League and is a member of the PCL Hall of Fame.

# FAVORITE PCL "CHARACTER"

Only a select few could compare with former major league pitcher **Chester "Chesty Chet" Johnson** when it comes to League "characters." His delightful antics endeared this man to fans all over the Coast League. His little black book on how to pitch batters, along with the coonskin cap which he often wore while hitting, were beautifully woven into his act. He also quite often came to the plate with a broom for a bat. The umpires usually allowed him to wave it back and forth a few times before making him pick up a bat and get down to the business of hitting.

Be advised that all his shenanigans took place during the course of a game, and were not some form of entertainment he provided before or after a league contest. This is what made him so unique. Chet's antics often befuddled opposing batters. So captivated by this man was I that I once skipped a wedding I should have attended to see him pitch. Believe me, the bride has never been friendly with me since, and over 28 years have elapsed.

My unofficial records indicate that Johnson played with five PCL teams—Seattle, San Diego, San Francisco, Oakland and

**Chet Johnson**

Sacramento. In the seven seasons between 1950 and 1956 he won 71 games, while losing 87. It should be pointed out that in those seven seasons his earned run average was above 3.00 only two times. His best season was 1950, when his record was 22–13 while pitching for San Francisco.

Even though he had a losing record, he was a winner with everyone who ever saw him play. I will never forget this man and the things he did to bring joy and happiness to Pacific Coast League fans. Everybody loved him and most players went along with his humor. Chet passed away April 10, 1983, in Seattle.

## FAVORITE PCL UMPIRE

Can there be any doubt who would be my choice for favorite Coast League umpire? It can only be the late **Emmett Ashford**. His dramatic gestures when making a call, coupled with his exaggerated head movements and peculiar method of running backwards when taking his position as a base umpire, distinguished him from all others. Beyond all of that, he was an accurate and decisive umpire and a credit to the profession. Can you imagine how much fun fans must have had when Bobby Bragan, Chet Johnson and Emmett Ashford were involved in the same game? I personally never saw this combination, but I'm certain it came up.

Ashford was the first black umpire in the Pacific Coast League and he served as Umpire-in-Chief of the PCL before the American League purchased his contract.

Although I have no proof, I'm firm in the opinion that the American League wrongfully censured some of Ashford's mannerisms. Both he and American League fans were the worse for it. If he was competent in his work, and he surely was, why force a man out of character? The point to be made is that many times I saw at work in the PCL a relaxed, refreshing and totally capable umpire.

Emmett Ashford was the best umpire I've seen in the Coast League, and one of the best I've seen in any league.

# MOST SUCCESSFUL PLAYER IN THE SHORTEST TIME

**Steve Bilko** came to the PCL in 1955 and played first base with the Los Angeles Angels through the 1957 season. During that three-year stretch, he thoroughly dominated the League. Those three years unquestionably belonged to the big man from Pennsylvania. He never hit under .300 and his .360 batting average in 1956 led the League. If this accomplishment was not enough, he displayed tremendous power, leading the League in home runs all three years. He hit 37 homers in 1955, 55 in 1956, and 56 in 1957, for a grand total of 148.

I realize that some of you might raise the question of the shortness of Wrigley Field's left field wall, but you and I know Steve didn't hit all of his round trippers at Wrigley Field. This man had the power to rip the ball out of any park. It is a fact that he many times cleared the walls of every PCL stadium.

Let's go on—he led the League in RBI's two of his three years in the PCL. He was nudged out of the RBI lead in 1955 by another favorite of mine, outfielder Earl Rapp of San Diego. In his three years, Bilko drove in 428 runs. He demonstrated his three-year dominance of the League by being named its most valuable player all three years, a Coast League record.

Without demeaning PCL hurlers or detracting from Bilko's accomplishments, the cliche we've all used that hitters see good pitching every day in the majors, but not day-by-day in the minors, proved to be accurate in the case of Steve Bilko. He played with several major league teams before and after his PCL days and found the going less than easy. Although this is true, nothing could diminish Steve Bilko's baseball successes in the PCL. He was the most successful player in the shortest period of time that I ever saw play in the Pacific Coast League!

# MOST COURAGEOUS PLAYER

**Joe Sprinz** was second only to Billy Raimondi among catchers that impressed me in the PCL. He was catching in the League with San Francisco when I became a fan in 1938. He remained with the Seals through the 1946 season, after which he retired. His best year with the bat was 1939, when he hit .312. It is my opinion that he and Bruggie Ogrodowski formed the best catching tandem of any pair of receivers assembled during my time.

Although 1939 was Joe's best year with the bat that I have record of, it was perhaps his worst year with the ball. Here's what I mean: He and several of his San Francisco teammates went over to Treasure Island during the 1939 World's Fair with the idea of catching a baseball dropped from a Goodyear blimp. When the people in the blimp were ready to drop the ball, only Sprinz remained with enough courage to attempt this dangerous feat.

Three balls were dropped. The first one went into the stands. The second ball was difficult to see and it fell to the ground. The third ball he saw all the way and it was coming extremely fast. Joe relates how he shielded his eyes from the sun with his mitt as

the ball bore down on him. The ball hit him in the mouth knocking him to the ground, though he did not lose consciousness. He was taken to Saint Joseph's Hospital, where numerous stitches were taken, as were X-rays. They revealed eleven cracks in his upper jaw. In all, he spent three months in the hospital. Upon being released, his teeth were wired, as they were badly out of alignment, and for two additional months he could only take liquids and soft foods.

The following quotes reveal Joe's feelings before and after the accident:

> When the blimp came over the field, I was the only one to stand, and the rest left, so it was up to me. I said to myself, God hates a coward, so I was it.

> When Spring training came, I took soccer shoes with me and caught batting every day. Also had the coach hit high pop fouls. Also did a lot of praying for courage.

For years I have coveted the information straight from the "horse's mouth" regarding this courageous incident. Thanks to the kindness of Joe Sprinz, you and I both now have it.

# MOST LEARNED PLAYER

I have always had the highest regard for the well-rounded individual. When a person is a good student and a good athlete as well, that to me is fantastic. And such a person is **Ed "Fiddler/Professor" Basinski** of the Portland Beavers. Basinski graduated from the University of Buffalo with a Bachelor of Science Degree. He is an accomplished violinist, having been a regular member of the Buffalo Symphony Orchestra. You don't attain that position by "sawing out an old ditty" I understand that Ed also plays piano and enjoys singing.

He broke into professional baseball with the Brooklyn Dodgers in 1944 directly from the amateur ranks. He also appeared in 56 games with the Pittsburgh Pirates before coming to the Coast League, where I remember him for at least 11 seasons (1947–57). I could belabor you with statistics, but be assured he was an excellent glove man and a good steady hitter.

I chose Basinski as the second baseman on my PCL All-Star team, although I must give recognition to Hugh Luby, who likewise was an excellent second baseman and a good hitter during my time. Basinski and Luby had many pluses, and this was a tough decision for me to make. It's my opinion that Jimmy Reese from earlier years, Ed Basinski, and Hugh Luby were the top three among second sackers who played in the PCL over an extended period of time.[*]

We are seeing quite a bit of the educated athlete in professional sports nowadays. It was, however, much more of a rarity in the '40s and '50s. Believe me when I say I really looked up to Ed Basinski.

It would boost my stock if I could tell you I was out of the Basinski mold. Yes, I have a degree and played around at sports, and in fact played third trumpet in the high school band. But compared to Ed Basinski, I never really "knowed" what it was all about.

---

[*]Luby and Basinski both had long consecutive game streaks which together totaled 1,423 contests. Luby's streak was from 1938 to 1943, Basinski's from 1949 to 1952.

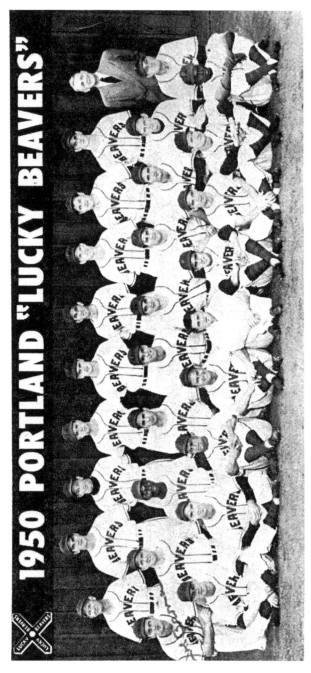

# 1950 PORTLAND "LUCKY BEAVERS"

**PORTLAND "LUCKY BEAVERS" – 1950 SEASON**

Top Row, Left to Right: Bill Sweeney, mgr; Jim Gladd, Bill Elbert, Johnny Rucker, Fenton Mole, Vince DeBiasi, "Red" Adams, Bill Fleming, Cal McIrvin, Bill Mulligan, gen. mgr. Middle Row: Joe Brovia, Roy Helser, Luis Marquez, Mickey Rocco, Ed Barr, Bob Drilling, Vic Mastro, Jack Creel, Ed Basinski, Art Mills, coach. Bottom Row: Lyman Linde, Hillis Layne, John Ritchey, Steve Mesner, "Tip" Berg, trainer; Leo Thomas, Dain Clay, "Red" Lynn, Frank Austin.

# MOST UNUSUAL PITCHER

There have been and still are many variations in the way pitchers deliver baseballs. Generally speaking, they range from directly over the top to three-quarters to those known as sidewinders. Rarely do we ever hear of the submarine pitcher, who whips the ball up to the plate in semi-softball style. I can remember only one in the Pacific Coast League, the great Portland right-hander **Ad Liska**.

Liska pitched many years in the League and was pitching when I first became a fan. Portland was the only Coast League team he played for. He was with the Beavers from 1936 to 1949, and won a total of 248 minor league games and lost 229. One hundred ninety-eight of those victories were with Portland.

Liska's style of pitching was most interesting to observe and required a pronounced adjustment on the part of opposing batters who were used to seeing the ball come to the plate in a general downward trajectory. It is only supposition, but I've often thought that if Liska had been pitching today he might have been used primarily in relief. By the time batters adjusted to his style, he could have held a lead or squelched an uprising a high percentage of the time.

Be that as it may, Liska was a great starting pitcher in the Coast League and, in my opinion, was foremost among submarine pitchers of any era, including contemporary submariner Ted Ahernathy.

Before going on, I feel compelled to state right here that I am sticking to my earlier statement that Ad Liska was the only submarine pitcher that I recall in the PCL. I say this fully realizing that some of you may ask, "What about Sam Gibson?" I am personally of the opinion that Sam would better be described as a sidewinder. Numerous worry warts throughout the League displayed great concern for the well-being of Liska's knuckles, since his phalanges came ever so close to scraping the mound every time he delivered a pitch. No such anxiety was demonstrated when Sam Gibson threw the ball plateward. Gibson was one of the League's most imposing hurlers, but I believe he achieved greatness by being a super, intimidating

sidewinder. If you disagree, I still think you are a fantastic, wonderful person. After all, you proved that by purchasing this capricious literary masterpiece.

Ad Liska completed 21 years of minor league service. During that time his combined ERA was 3.37. In 1943, he had a super earned-run average, 1.98. That same year he pitched in 254 innings. In the 12 years that I followed his career, he appeared in 30 or more games 10 times, his highest being 46 in 1938. He won 20 games twice during my time, 20–16 in 1939 and 20–12 in 1945. Liska played in 666 minor league games, 426 between the years of 1938 and 1949.

## MOST PRODIGIOUS THROW

I spoke earlier of the various contests that took place before PCL games. One such contest that I personally enjoyed was the throwing-for-accuracy contest. The contestants would throw from a point in center field to home plate, with each player allowed four or five throws. I've seen some super accurate tosses, and likewise I've observed some mighty errant flings. The throw I'm about to describe would, I guess, come under the errant classification, although it really was straight-on.

**Jackie Jensen**, one day at Oaks Park in the late '40s, uncorked a throw that not only made it to home plate but far beyond. The ball sailed over the backstop screen, which itself was quite high, and hit the base of the press box, bringing the scribes and announcers out of the box in headscratching bewilderment. Conservatively, the ball carried over 400 feet on the fly. Although this is not a story of earthshaking magnitude, it does prove that Jensen was a complete player. His hitting successes and ability as an outfielder are well known. This little narration proved that he had a great arm.

Jensen was a very confident baseball player and made no bones about the fact that he, not Mickey Mantle, should have been the heir to Joe DiMaggio's center field job with the Yankees.

# MOST ADEPT AT
# HITTING HOME RUNS

There were many great sluggers in the PCL during my time, but none, to my knowledge, hit more round trippers than big **Frank Kelleher**. In twelve seasons, he belted 234 homers, which played a big part in his driving in 876 runs. Twice he led the Coast League in home runs. He hit a League-leading 29 in 1944, his first year with Hollywood, and in 1950 he led the circuit with 40 homers.

Frank used a modified Mel Ott approach to hitting (front leg raised) and it was indeed successful. Not only was he one of the League's most prolific long ball hitters, but he carried a minor league batting average of .282, which is quite good for a free swinger who all too often sacrificed points from his average.

I must tell you that I agonized greatly before deciding not to put Kelleher on my PCL All-Star Team. I can truthfully say, though, that I am at peace with my selections.

Hollywood was blessed with its share of power hitters, men like Babe Herman, Gus Zernial and Dale Long, but Frank Kelleher was special to me. Frank passed away in April of 1973, but his memory will always live in the hearts of everyone who saw him play.

# MOST ADEPT AT
# HITTING FEWEST HOMERS

If you're looking for the long ball, **Billy Raimondi** is not your man. Statistically speaking (that sounds most impressive coming from me), you could expect him to clear the boards approximately one time in every 575 trips to the plate. This meant that Oakland fans were totally unfamiliar with his home run trot. In twenty years of PCL play, he never hit more than one round tripper in a season, with the exception of 1945 when he blasted two out of the park. This feat apparently burned him out, though, since he never homered again the rest of his career, which lasted eight more years. He homered in only six of his twenty years in the PCL, and in all he hit only seven Coast League home runs.

Well, even though we've had some fun with his record, I want to make it clear that to me and many others Billy Raimondi was the best catcher who ever played in the Pacific Coast League. Including two years in the Arizona–Texas League, his minor league batting average was .276, and he played 2,292 minor league games from 1931 to 1953. Some of you older fans remember that Billy was extremely successful in throwing runners out at second base without leaving the crouch. Quite honestly, I can remember no other catcher who did this.

* * * *

It occurs to me that after having had a little amusement with Billy Raimondi, this is a good place to pause and attempt to clear the air, should there be any misunderstanding. Although you may not get the impression (I hope I'm wrong), how a player performed while playing the game was paramount with me. Shenanigans, horseplay, interesting incidents on or off the field are more a part of baseball than any other sport, and how I dearly love to write on the subject of trivia! But, I can think of no one that I poked fun at in this book who was not an excellent baseball player and a great human being.

Remember this as a rule of thumb: *Nobody ever teases someone that he doesn't truly like!* ...Now, let's get back to the subject at hand.

# MOST VERSATILE

The versatile baseball player in the PCL was not a rarity. The multi-purpose player has always been around. He was particularly in evidence during the war years, being thrust into several positions, of necessity more often than not.

Quite frankly, I can remember no player who made radical position changes who achieved *great* success, but since I do want to make mention of this subject, I will start with the first player I remember who did successfully change positions.

I first remember **Al Libke** as a pitcher for Seattle in 1942 and as a first baseman/outfielder in 1944. I then remember him as an outfielder with Hollywood in 1947 and 1948. Libke's best year with the bat was 1947, when he hit .310 with ten home runs and 81 RBI's. He, along with **Ed Carnett** of Seattle, were the first players I remember who combined pitching with the outfield and first base.

There are four other men I'd like to make mention of under this subject. The first two are outfielders **Al Lyons** and **Tom Hafey**, who became pitchers. I remember Lyons as a relief pitcher with Hollywood. Hafey was at one time in the Oakland rotation, along with his brother Will. The other two are **Paul Pettit**, who switched from pitching to the outfield and first base, and **Ray Orteig**, who was formerly a San Francisco third baseman. Orteig gave up the hot corner and was converted to a catcher while still at San Francisco. He later caught for Seattle. Of these four, Ray Orteig was the most outstanding, in my opinion, doing a fine job at both positions. He was always a good hitter. By the way, it seemed to me that Seattle successfully converted, or simply had, more players who changed from one position to another than any other PCL club.

**AL LIBKE**
Pitcher, first baseman, outfielder – Seattle, early 1940s
Outfielder – Hollywood, 1947–48

*"Many pitchers are excellent athletes and could be either good hitters or good pitchers, or both. Many of us played several positions because we were able to adapt."*

Well, it doesn't end here, but I really believe the players I'm going to list next should come under the title of *Versatility in Reverse*. Would you believe that such great infielders as **Les Scarsella**, **Ed Basinski**, **Buck Faucett**, **Jack Lohrke** and **Dale Long** all took a shot at pitching somewhere along the line? Outfielder **Marv Gudat** even threw a few plateward, as did **Johnny Lindell**. With Lindell it was no joke. He was good with the bat and as a pitcher. If memory serves me well, he succeeded as a knuckleball pitcher with Hollywood somewhere around 1951 and 1952. Lindell had also done some pitching in the PCL years earlier.

Getting back to the subject of versatility in reverse, there was one who stood head and shoulders above all others in this regard. **Carlos Bernier**, although an excellent outfielder, had no more business being on the infield than your grandmother. Carlos played 67 games at third base for Hollywood in 1955 and had next to the lowest fielding percentage in the League, .883. Bernier's being positioned at third did give the Stars a good bat, since Bobby Bragan was caught short at that position by the return to the majors of regular third sacker George Freese.

Perhaps we've had more fun than fact while on the subject of versatility. We did, however, see a good bit of it in the League. There are, of course, still some of these players around today, but let's face it—we are living in an age of specialization…baseball included.

# MOST INTENSE PLAYER

It should be obvious by now that I have a penchant for the "character" or "flake," be they players, managers or umpires. At the same time, there is no place in baseball, by my standards, for anyone who will not put everything he has into the game. Natural ability is not enough!

Foremost among players that I remember who possessed ability and intense desire was **Gene Mauch**, former L.A. Angel second baseman. This man ranks high on my list as a student of the game (Ted Williams is No. 1). Mauch's formula could only mean success, and for him it meant just that. I got the feeling that he had no friends during the course of a game. Whatever it took to win, that's what he did. As a successful manager, I'm certain he expects no less than this from his players.

Mauch was satisfied to play in the Coast League. He once signed a contract waiving any possibility of returning to the majors. I'm glad, however, that he was able to go back to the big leagues later on with Boston.

As an added personal note, I had one short occasion to talk with Mauch on my trip to Oakland in 1955. I happened out of Tiny's Coffee Shop at the same time he was heading back to the Leamington Hotel. Yes, I was there to see Hollywood play, but the Angels had just finished a series with the Oaks and were not leaving until the next morning. My buddy Lloyd and I made the most of those few blocks from restaurant to hotel. Little did I know at that time that this man would be one of baseball's most astute managers. Really, though, I'm not surprised; he possessed all the ingredients that went into making a fine player and field general, as well.

# MOST VOLATILE PLAYER

This could only be **Carlos Bernier**. He was a most exciting ball player to watch; I really liked this guy. Bernier was one of those fiery Latins who had great difficulty containing himself when things weren't going well. He never liked being called out on strikes or being thrown out attempting to steal a base. Since he felt this way, he simply made his feelings known to one and all.

Many, many times I've seen him have to be restrained. This then made him angry at his own players, who were only trying to calm him down. You can imagine how the fans got on him, especially when one of these incidents happened on the road. I remember well how he handled this. He turned his head in the direction where he was being blistered the most and spat a fine stream of saliva at his detractors. This had to be made possible by a rather large opening between his two upper front teeth.

Make no mistake about it, Bernier was an excellent player. He was a good defensive outfielder and above-average hitter.

Although my records do not go beyond 1957, it should be pointed out that Bernier led the Coast League in hitting in 1961 with an average of .351.

One cannot talk about Carlos Bernier without mentioning his excellent speed, which not only made him a good outfielder but also a premier base stealer. I admit I may not have been with it when it came to being up on those who were adept at stealing bases in the League. I doubt, however, that there were too many who could have topped this man. Bernier had 594 minor league thefts. He stole 192 of these at Hollywood. He led minor league circuits six times; three times he led the PCL.*

I thoroughly enjoyed watching Carlos play. Remember, most quick-tempered people are also the warm, friendly type. Carlos Bernier was this kind of man. I've seen his broad smile many times.

# MOST LENGTHY NAME

**Calvin Coolidge Julius Caesar Tecumseh McLish** is the real name of former Angel and Padre pitcher we all knew as just Cal McLish. I remember hearing several broadcasters query McLish regarding his lengthy name, but I have no recollection of his mentioning the reason for these various names being selected. I'm angry at myself for not paying closer attention during those interviews. I do recall that much conversation went into the length of the name, rather than the origin.

McLish began with the Brooklyn Dodgers as a 19-year-old rookie. He spent two stints in the Coast League, beginning with the Angels in 1949 and 1950. He went up to the Cubs in 1951, but a losing season found him back with Los Angeles in 1952. He played with the Angels for three years and was traded to San Diego for the 1955 campaign. He won 56 games during those four years. He went back to the majors and was in the starting rotation of the Cleveland Indians where he had two good years.

---

*Bill Ramsey of Seattle was another fleet base runner. I have him unofficially with 205 PCL stolen bases. He was often involved in foot race contests around the League. Frenchy Uhalt also had over 200 stolen bases and led the PCL in steals in 1938.

McLish is still active as a major league pitching coach and has served under several managers.

# MOST EMBARRASSING INCIDENT

The interesting part of this incident I'm about to relate was that it directly involved the manager. Skipper Bobby Bragan was catching and utility infielder Jack Lohrke was playing third base. I fail to remember whether Bragan was trying to pick a runner off of third or simply threw down there after a batter struck out. At any rate, Lohrke's thoughts were not in the ballpark (perhaps he was enjoying a pleasant day on Waikiki). He looked up just in time to feel the ball hit him squarely above the left eye.

Even though it had to hurt, what possible excuse could one offer for not keeping his head in the game, especially when his manager was just 90 feet away? I saw Lohrke a few days after that; sunglasses were the order of the day—and of the night. He looked for sure as if he had taken a blow from the reigning heavyweight champ. This incident could have been more serious, since Lohrke always wore prescription glasses when he played.

# MOST MIRACULOUS RECOVERY

It is a fact that the Coast League was well known for its quality of players and officials, but it had to be known for having at least one miracle-working trainer. I don't know who this gentleman was, but I well remember the result of his "magic." The San Diego Padres were at Gilmore Field and their second baseman **Al Federoff** was at the plate. He swung at a pitch and went down in a heap in total agony—a knee injury. He slowly struggled to his feet, and using the bat as a cane finally got back to the San Diego dugout on the third base line. In my mind's eye I visualized some decrepit old man trying to make it to his favorite, well-worn rocking chair.

Only a few minutes elapsed when a man came running out of the San Diego dugout headed for home plate. I thought it was a pinch hitter, but to my utter surprise it was Al Federoff, good as new, ready to resume hitting. He finished the game without a limp, and as far as I know finished the season and his career without any further problems with that knee.

With regard to trainers, I can only remember one PCL trainer, that being "Freddie" Frederico, who was with Seattle. Most of us in Southern California remember Frederico as the ranking American League trainer, having begun with the Los Angeles/California Angels in 1961. He retired, but it was short-lived. He went back to work with the Milwaukee Brewers.

Worthy of note is the fact that former Hollywood first baseman Tony Bartirome is the current trainer of the Pittsburgh Pirates.*

# MOST DANGEROUS STADIUM

Lane Field in San Diego was an interesting old stadium which was located at the junction of Broadway and the old Pacific Coast Highway. The proximity of its right field wall to the Coast Highway was what made this venerable ball yard so perilous. If memory serves me correctly, only a sidewalk separated the fence from the highway. I really doubt that there is any way to find out how much damage was done over the years to the windshields and hoods of the many vehicles plunked by baseballs ripped out of the park by power hitting left-handed batters.

Just for fun, I looked up the number of homers hit by Max West, Jack Graham and Earl Rapp when they wore Padre livery.† These long-ball lefties combined for 354 home runs. I would imagine that a majority of those round trippers were hit at Lane Field. Now, combine these homers with the home runs hit by other Padre and visiting teams' portside swingers, and you had to have an insurance adjuster's nightmare. Well, I guess it was drive at your own risk. Closing the Coast Highway for a Padre

---

*Bartirome was a fancy fielding first baseman who caught every ball with one hand. He was by no means a "showboat" and never advocated that youngsters copy his style.

†Did not all play for San Diego at the same time.

game in those days would be like shutting down one of today's freeways—it just couldn't be done.*

## MOST BEAUTIFUL STADIUM

Of the teams which were in the League from 1938 to 1957, I have seen baseball games in all but four stadiums—Lucky

**WRIGLEY FIELD · LOS ANGELES, CALIFORNIA**

---

*Much damage was also done to windows of homes located just over the left field wall at Wrigley Field.

Beaver Stadium and Multnomah Stadium in Portland, Sick's Stadium in Seattle, and Capilano Stadium in Vancouver, British Columbia, Canada. **Wrigley Field** in Los Angeles was, to me, the best. This was a double-decked stadium from foul pole to foul pole. It also had a bleacher section in right center field. I'm told the park was patterned after Wrigley Field in Chicago, but on a smaller scale. I'm quite certain that Wrigley Field was far superior in every respect to most major league parks.

That statement is not far-fetched when you consider the many major league stadiums that either had to be rebuilt or remodeled. To me, Wrigley was unquestionably the class of all PCL parks. Its ivy-covered outfield walls, its bleacher section and elaborate scoreboard added greatly to its beauty. Even though this marvelous stadium could seat 25,000, it appeared to me to have a cozy atmosphere. Angel broadcasters and the news media referred to it as "beautiful Wrigley Field"—and truly it was.

## PCL ALL-STAR LINEUP

Well, I've put off inserting my All-Star lineups as long as I can. Maybe I'm fearful some of you old-timers will disagree sharply with me. I realize that when one attempts to name any all-star lineup he is open to criticism and disagreement. I will doubtless be no exception. All those I have listed were established, solid players, and I sincerely believe I have been objective in the selection of these men.

After spending considerable time in thinking over, then writing down the names of those I felt should receive mention as all-star candidates, I abandoned the idea and opted to go with the starting eight only, plus one right- and one left-handed pitcher. The more I wrote, the more sentiment clouded my thinking; I simply couldn't do it justice. Incidentally, should you raise the question as to why such former PCL greats as Jigger Statz and Frank Shellenback are not in my lineup, the answer is simple.

Even though they appeared during my 20-year PCL involvement (Shellenback only one year as a manager, 1938), it was too short a period of time for them to qualify under the guidelines I established for selecting my PCL All-Star Team.

My lineup was selected after personally seeing players perform over an extensive period of time in the Coast League. They doubtless would appear on any all-time PCL all-star team. Jigger Statz could not be overlooked on my L.A. Angel all-star team. He had impressive statistics at an older age covering the five-year period from 1938 to 1942.

These twelve all-stars, which include the manager and coach, combined for 149 years of PCL service, not to mention the years before 1938. The individual years played ranged from a high of sixteen to a low of nine. Here goes…

# The 12 ALL-STARS of the PACIFIC COAST LEAGUE

| YEARS | |
|---|---|
| 10 | **"KEWPIE DICK" BARRETT** <br> Right-Handed Pitcher • WON 170/LOST 124 |
| 10 | **TONY FREITAS** <br> Left-Handed Pitcher • WON 155/LOST 129 |
| 16 | **BILLY RAIMONDI** <br> Catcher • .274 |
| 9 | **LES SCARSELLA** <br> First Base • .302 |
| 11 | **EDDIE BASINSKI** <br> Second Base • .260 |
| 9 | **HARVEY STOREY** <br> Third Base • .279 |
| 10 | **BILLY SCHUSTER** <br> Shortstop • .277 |
| 11 | **JOE BROVIA** <br> Outfield • .305 |
| 9 | **EARL RAPP** <br> Outfield • .318 |
| 14 | **BROOKS HOLDER** <br> Outfield • .294 |
| 20 | **FRANK "LEFTY" O'DOUL** <br> Manager |
| 20 | **JIMMY REESE** <br> Coach |

# PCL ALL-STARS

# QUICKIE ALL-STAR STATS
## (Unofficial)

The starting eight, exclusive of the pitchers, combined for 39,936 at-bats, 11,592 hits, for a team batting average of .290. They hit 750 home runs and had 5,814 RBI's. Brooks Holder had the most at-bats (7,131), most hits (2,100) and RBI's (855). Joe Brovia had the most home runs, 174. Earl Rapp had the highest batting average, .318. And Billy Raimondi played the longest, 16 years. (He played an additional four years previous to 1938.)

# ALL-STAR SELECTIONS
# BY TEAMS

My criterion for selecting all-stars was that they must have played with their respective teams no less than three years. This did not have to necessarily occur consecutively. I felt this was a good method of making the selections more accurate and meaningful. I expected to have little difficulty in meeting this criterion, and for the most part this was true.

I must tell you, however, that there were a few exceptions. So few were they, that I will leave it at that without further comment. I believe I have been objective in selecting the overwhelming majority of these team all-stars, but do admit to some sentimental choices. I am not attempting to name an all-star team from Vancouver, since they were only in the League two years during the period of which I write (see *Oakland All-Star Team*).

**HOLLYWOOD**

| | | |
|---|---|---|
| George "Pinky" Woods - P | Chuck Stevens - 1st B | Tod Davis - SS |
| Mike Sandlock - C | Gene Handley - 2nd B | Frank Kelleher - OF |
| | Jack Phillips - 3rd B | "Frenchy" Uhalt - OF |
| | | Carlos Bernier - OF |

**LOS ANGELES**

| | | |
|---|---|---|
| "Red" Lynn - P | Steve Bilko - 1st B | Billy Schuster - SS |
| Billy Holm - C | Gene Mauch - 2nd B | Jigger Statz - OF |
| | Charlie English - 3rd B | Lou Novikoff - OF |
| | | Cecil Garriott - OF |

## OAKLAND

Cotton Pippen - P     Les Scarsella - 1st B     Ray Hamrick - SS
Billy Rairnondi - C     Hugh Luby - 2nd B     George Metkovich - OF
    "Spider" Jorgenson - 3rd B     Marv Gudat - OF
    Loyd Christopher - OF

## PORTLAND

Ad Liska - P     Herm Reich - 1st B     Frankie Austin - SS
Jim Gladd - C     Eddie Basinski - 2nd B     Joe Brovia - OF
    Harvey Storey - 3rd B     Johnny Gill - OF
    Spencer Harris - OF

## SACRAMENTO

Tony Freitas - P     "Nippy" Jones - 1st B     Eddie Lake - SS
Ed Fitzgerald - C     Joe Gordon - 2nd B     Bob Dillinger - OF
    Steve Mesner - 3rd B     Joe Marty - OF
    Al Heist - OF

## SAN FRANCISCO

Sam Gibson - P     Ferris Fain - 1st B     Roy Nicely - SS
Joe Sprinz - C     Jim Moran - 2nd B     Brooks Holder - OF
    Ted Jennings - 3rd B     Ted Norbert - OF
    Dino Restelli - OF

## SAN DIEGO

Herm Pillette - P     Jack Graham - 1st B     "Buddy" Peterson - SS
George Detore - C     Al Federoff - 2nd B     Earl Rapp - OF
    Mike Haslin - 3rd B     Max West - OF
    Clarence Maddern - OF

## SEATTLE

"Kewpie Dick" Barrett - P     Earl Torgeson - 1st B     Artie Wilson - SS
Ray Orteig - C     Al Niemiec- 2nd B     Jo Jo White - OF
    Dick Gyselman - 3rd B     Bill Lawrence - OF
    Bill Ramsey - OF

# PCL WOMEN'S
# ALL-STAR TEAM

While on the subject of all-star teams, and considerably on the lighter side, if women had played in the PCL might the following have been on the League's all-star team? I trust no one will take umbrage with me on this; it is meant only in fun. Disregard some of the positions given. (You might even want to disregard the whole thing.)

Gail Henley - CF
Fay Thomas - SS
Fern Bell - RF
Francis Kelleher - LF
Nellie King - 1st B
Cleo Carlyle - 3rd B
Jean Roy - 2nd B
Marion Tobin - C
Connie Dempsey - P

B. Joyce - Manager
A. Lilly - Coach

# FINAL GAME
# SAN FRANCISCO STYLE

One familiar characteristic of the PCL in my day was the way it closed its season (last game), especially when the championship had already been decided and/or a team had no chance of moving up in the standings. They simply threw convention out the window and had a real ball. Everyone got into the act. Both the players and the fans were extremely loose, and I doubt that there were any PCL teams that didn't at some point in time participate in one of these nothing-to-lose or nothing-to-gain games.

Let me tell you of one such game before adding some more of my highly intellectual, yet discursive comments (it's great to be free from the worry that the author might be up for a literary award). The game I want to talk about took place in 1957 at Seals' Stadium in San Francisco and involved the Seals and the Sacramento Solons. It was the second game of a double-header and the last PCL game ever played in the fabled uncovered stadium. San Francisco had already won the pennant and the Seals' fine infielder, Ken Aspromonte, was the batting champ, with an average of .334. This meant that all the Seals' players were loose, and Sacramento—who had a firm grip on seventh place—was equally free from restraint.

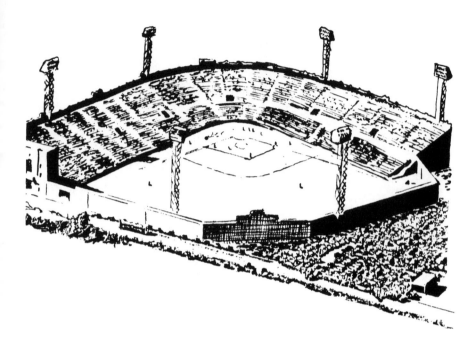

**SEALS' STADIUM · SAN FRANCISCO, CALIFORNIA**

Should you picture in your mind a Marx brothers matinee set in a ball field, you would probably still fall short of the hilarity that transpired that fall Sunday afternoon in San Francisco. The main characters were Seals' manager Joe Gordon and home plate umpire Chris Pelekoudas. Gordon opened the game at his usual position of second base and it seemed as though the game would be played straight, as was game one of the double-header. Pretty soon, however, players began appearing in unfamiliar positions and the game began to fall apart. Gordon, desiring to show his versatility, took to the mound and immediately proved that he made a right decision years earlier not to seek fame or fortune as a pitcher.

Before too much time had elapsed, umpire Pelekoudas began riding Gordon to the extent that the manager asked the ump if he could do any better. Chris said he believed he could, whereupon he took off the umpire's gear and replaced Gordon on the hill. By that time the fans were getting into the frivolous spirit of things, and numerous beer parties began breaking out all over the stadium.

Finally, little Albie Pearson ended up on the mound for San Francisco, after having already played four different positions. He had the dubious distinction of serving up the last home run ball ever pitched at Seals' Stadium by a member of a Coast League team. I don't know who hit that homer, but nobody really knew or cared. Needless to say, the records of this game were thrown out, denying Sacramento a sweep of the twin bill. There were 15,484 fans in attendance for that farewell double-header.

Incidentally, if you equate the individual "comedy" engaged in by numerous Coast League players during the course of a campaign with the last game of the season horseplay, you are wrong in that evaluation. Although fans throughout the League enjoyed what they saw, it was all done for a purpose; namely, to shake up the opposition.

Well, this game in San Francisco might well have been the most hilarious of all the closing-day games, but I kind of believe that players and fans collectively were covering up their true melancholy feelings, knowing that PCL baseball was forever over in the Bay Area and Los Angeles.

My personal sentiments can best be described in the words of this song from yesteryear, *"Laughing on the outside, crying on the inside."*

*"Lefty Joe" Hatten Is All Right.*

# NICKNAMES

I recently read an article where the writer was lamenting the fact that many great nicknames in sports are becoming a thing of the past, particularly in baseball. After meditating on this for a while I sadly agree it is true. In trying to understand why this has become a reality, one must ask: What gives rise to nicknames in the first place? There are several reasons, beginning with the fact that it was the popular thing to do for many, many years. Other reasons range from the covering up of a distasteful given name, to the color of one's hair, to the shape of one's nose, to some peculiar personal mannerism.

I believe that most people like their nicknames, or can at least tolerate a "handle" someone has thrust on them. We do, however, occasionally hear of those whose nicknames stuck, but they nonetheless hated them. Before going on with some more thoughts on this interesting subject, allow me to tell you of one gentleman who detested his nickname, although it was with him for years. This story does not involve a Coast Leaguer, but it does involve a former baseball player.

Ex-New York Yankee great Charlie Keller was dubbed "King Kong," I believe around the time the famous movie was made. Even though, I assume, it was intended as a compliment indicating Keller's great strength, he never liked it and never wanted to hear it. New York broadcaster Phil Rizzuto tells the story of how he personally caught the wrath of one Charlie "King Kong" Keller.

Baseball players, as you know, are forever pulling stunts, especially where rookies are concerned. Rizzuto tells of the time when he joined the Yankees as a raw-boned, innocent rookie and was anxious to please all the veterans, Keller included. One rascal teammate told Rizzuto that if he wanted to get on the good side of Charlie Keller, the best way to do it was to call him "King Kong," the more times the better. Rizzuto appreciated the advice and did just that. Before he knew what happened, he was several feet off the ground, being slammed into the lockers by a furious Charlie Keller. Can't you just visualize a terrified little Phil Rizzuto with a look of disbelief written all over his face, while receiving an animated lecture from his adversary? Rizzuto said he could laugh about it now, but he was one frightened rookie at that time.

Is there a number one reason why nicknames are given? I suppose not. I do think, though, that one major reason is to cover up for parental blundering in the selection of names. Junior at some point either selected or accepted a nickname, rather than bringing himself to confront the old man as to what brand of booze he was drinking when a name was agreed upon, especially if that name happened to be Rufus, Egbert, Horace or Horatio. The use of an acceptable nickname got mom and dad off the hook, and Junior could circulate freely without having to constantly explain his absurd appellation.

Well, maybe there is a little less tippling in recent times when parents select names, but I believe it is simply true that more conventional names are being given, along with the fact that nicknames are not as popular as they once were. Regardless of the reasons for their decline. I miss them. Those who know me are keenly aware I'll hang a nickname on anyone if given the chance. I do, however, confess I'm sensitive about my own name. I was born William Kendall Stadler, and it logically figured that I'd be called Bill. What could be so bad about that? But it so happened that from the beginning I was called Kendall. I strongly dislike it and have tried for my over 50 years to at least get it shortened down to *Ken*. In spite of all my efforts, there are those who still call me Kendall, no matter my protests.

It's incredible just how much nicknames became a part of some of these players on the list that follows. I honestly didn't know who some of them were when seeing their given names only. This should give you an idea of how nicknames were so much a part of many of these men.

Charles RED Adams
George SPARKY Anderson
Rinaldo RUGGER Ardizoia
Tracey KEWPIE DICK Barrett
Romanus MONTY Basgall
Ed FIDDLER/PROFESSOR Basinski
Dimitrios JIM Baxes
Walter WALLY Berger
Carlos BANDIT/COMET Bernier
JITTERY Joe Berry
STOUT Steve Bilko
Hiran HI Bithorn
Ewell WHIP Blackwell
Darrell CY Blanton
Robert BUD Blattner
Seymour CY Block
SONNY Jim Bolger
Bernhard BENNY Borgman
Clairborne CLAY Bryant

Thomas O. TOD Davis
Bobby THE GREEK Del Greco
Cornelius CONNIE Dempsey
Jack COOKIE Devincenzi
Sylvester BLIX Donnelly
Solomon SOLLY Drake
Luscious LUKE Easter
Robert BUCK Faucett
Froilan NANNY Fernandez
Linus LONNIE Frey
Fred HARD LUCK Gay
Al COWBOY Gettel
SAD Sam Gibson
Alban ALBIE Glossop
Jim MUDCAT Grant
Newton MICKEY Grasso
George MULE Haas
Lee JEEP Handley
J. Harrison TRUCK Hannah

Ora MICKEY Burnett
Ralph PINE TAR Buxton
Eldred BUD Byerly
John JAKE Caulfield
Emory BUBBA Church
Clarence CHUCK Churn
James RIP Collins
Rocco ROCKY Colavito
Kevin CHUCK Connors
Ellsworth BABE Dahlgren
DIM DOM Dominic Dallesandro
Harry HORSE Banning

Stanley BUCKY Harris
LEFTY Joe Hatten
Damon FIREBALL Hayes
Ralston ROLLIE Hemsley
Floyd BABE Herman
Clarence HOOKS Iott
Monford MONTY Irvin
Forrest SPOOK Jacobs
John SWEDE Jensen
Chester CHESTY CHET Johnson
Vernal NIPPY Jones
John SPIDER Jorgenson

REINDEER BILL Killefer
Nelson NELLIE King
Harry MOOSE Krause
Harry COOKIE Lavagetto
Adolph AD Liska
LUCKY Jack Lohrke
Ernie SNOOZE Lombardi
Omar TURK Lown
Harry PEANUTS Lowrey
Guillermo MEMO Luna
Ulysses TONY Lupien
Japhet RED Lynn
Garth RED Mann
Alfred BILLY Martin
John PEPPER Martin
George CAT/CATFISH Metkovich
Orestis MINNIE Minoso
Jacob JAKE Mooty
Cyril BUTCH Moran
George RED Munger
Gonzalo CHOLLY Naranjo
Rafael RAY Noblé
Ralph RUBE Novotney
Lou MAD RUSSIAN Novikoff
George EZRA O'Donnell
Frank LEFTY O'Doul
Ambrose BRUGGIE Ogrodowski
HANDY Andy Pafko
Ambrose BO Palica
Carl BUDDY Peterson
LOMITA LARRUPER Paul Pettit*
Herman OLD FOLKS Pillette
Henry COTTON Pippen

Marino CHIC Pieretti
SAILOR Bill Posedel
George BOBBY Prescott
Wellington WHIMPY Quinn
Xavier MISTER X Recigno
Manuel JIM Rivera
John HONEY Romano
Glen RIP Russell
Herman HAM Schulte
BROADWAY Billy Schuster
Kenny MINNIE MOUSE Sheehan
Hollis BUD Sheely
Frank SHELLY Shellenback
Harry SUITCASE Simpson
Dick SCOOTER Smith
George TUCK Stainback
Arnold JIGGER Statz
Charles Dillon CASEY Stengel
Glen GABBY Stewart
Dick SOCKO Stuart
August GUS Suhr
Matthew MAX Surkont
Wayne TWIG Terwilliger
Bernard FRENCHY Uhalt
Ben VIRGIL Wade
Joyner JO JO White
Weintraub MICKEY Winters
Kendall Cole CASEY Wise†
George RED Witt
George PINKY Woods
Al ZEKE Zarilla
Gus OZARK IKE Zemial

I selected the following names as the most logical to be covered up:

|            |           |
|------------|-----------|
| **Ambrose**    | **Japhet**    |
| **Cyril**      | **Ora**       |
| **Eldred**     | **Sylvester** |
| **Ellsworth**  | **Ulysses**   |
| **Emory**      | **Weintraub** |

*Paul Pettit was later named PILLS because of his interest in food supplement tablets. Fred Hutchinson hung that handle on him.

†Apparently Mr. Wise didn't like the name of Kendall either.

## SOME CATEGORICAL NICKNAMES

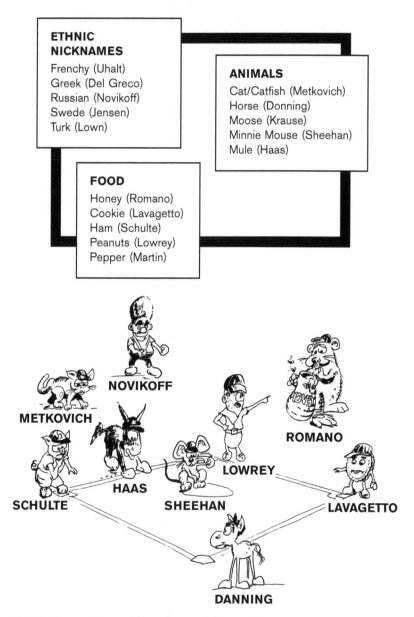

**ETHNIC NICKNAMES**
Frenchy (Uhalt)
Greek (Del Greco)
Russian (Novikoff)
Swede (Jensen)
Turk (Lown)

**ANIMALS**
Cat/Catfish (Metkovich)
Horse (Donning)
Moose (Krause)
Minnie Mouse (Sheehan)
Mule (Haas)

**FOOD**
Honey (Romano)
Cookie (Lavagetto)
Ham (Schulte)
Peanuts (Lowrey)
Pepper (Martin)

NOVIKOFF

METKOVICH

ROMANO

SCHULTE    HAAS    SHEEHAN    LOWREY    LAVAGETTO

DANNING

NOTE: Disregard the positions of some of these creatures.

# REASONS FOR NICKNAMES

I thought it might be of interest to give you the reasons and origin of some of the nicknames from my list, insofar as I know them. Needless to say, many are self-explanatory. I have, however, selected a few whose origins even some of you oldtimers may not know. But, especially for the younger readers who should chance to peruse these pages, I offer the following derivations:

### Carlos THE BANDIT/COMET Bernier

These nicknames were given to Bernier because of his speed and success at stealing bases. The word "bandit" fit well, since it was associated with the Mexican banditos. Bernier is a Latin.

### STOUT Steve Bilko

Bilko was not the sleek figure of a man we associate with most athletes (6'1", 240 lbs.); he was a large, robust individual who really could only have fit in in baseball as a pitcher or first baseman. The word "stout" fit him perfectly and flowed freely into his first name.

### Ralph "PINE TAR" Buxton

This nickname came up during my enjoyable contest with Rich Timmis and is the one and only occasion either of us remember any Coast League pitcher during our time who allegedly "greased up" a baseball. Whether Buxton actually used pine tar to make the ball do strange things we find hard to believe, since it would surely show up and thus give him away. If he did indeed "doctor" baseballs, we agree that he must have used a different substance, and the use of the word "pine tar" merely told everyone that Mr. Buxton was up to some "lubricatory" monkey business.*

---

*I suspect that old friend Bud Beasley was guilty of putting some moisture on baseballs, but have no proof. Something was going on during all his wild gyrations (windup) preparatory to sending the ball plateward.

## Thomas O. TOD Davis

In short, this nickname was given because the first letters of his three names formed the word "TOD." This nickname was always used when he played in the Coast League. He was known as "Tommy" while playing for the Philadelphia Athletics.

## Fred HARD LUCK Gay

Hollywood broadcasters began to refer to pitcher Fred Gay as "Hard Luck" because he would all too often lose ball games due to lack of support or poor hitting, or a combination of the two. I remember him and his plight in the early years.

## Al COWBOY Gettel

I don't believe this nickname was given to Gettel because he was an off-season wrangler, but because of his intense desire to play the cowhand. I remember Lefty O'Doul, while managing at Oakland, was very animated when bringing Gettel into the game as a relief pitcher. He would stand on the mound and mimic a galloping horse. Gettel knew that was the signal for him to enter the ballgame.

## Forrest SPOOK Jacobs

This nickname had nothing to do with goblins or ghosts, but was ascribed to Jacobs because of his ability to "spook" the ball just over the infielder's reach for base hits.

## LUCKY Jack Lohrke

If ever a nickname was appropriately given, this one was. Lohrke, on more than one occasion, was spared death or serious injury by some miraculous intervention.

## Ulysses TONY Lupien

This nickname was attached to Lupien because he had occasion to play on an all-Italian baseball team. Since it was necessary to be Italian in order to play, someone figured out a simple way to make this possible; they named him Tony. He was readily accepted and no problem ensued. I imagine public address announcers and radio broadcasters were most grateful for the selection of the nickname Tony, thereby not having to refer to Lupien as Ulysses.

### Alfred BILLY Martin

The name of Billy was given to Martin by his grandmother. The story is told that Billy didn't know his real first name until his first day of school. The teacher called the roll, and when she got to Billy he failed to respond to Alfred. When the teacher pursued the matter further, he steadfastly held to the fact that his name was Billy.

### George EZRA O'Donnell

This name was given to O'Donnell by his teammates. George was a tall, thin, slow-talking and slow-moving individual who players visualized perhaps as a character out of Li'l Abner. I remember O'Donnell both on and off the field. The nickname Ezra fit him well.

### Herman "OLD FOLKS" Pillette

This nickname was given to the great right-hander for two reasons. One was because he played in the PCL longer than any other player (23 years). The other reason was because he was just short of birthday number 48 when he finally hung up his cleats.

### BROADWAY Billy Schuster

The nickname "Broadway" was given to Bill Schuster by sports-writer Bob Hunter. It actually applied in two ways. First, Schuster was born in Buffalo, New York, one-half block off of Broadway. Secondly, the name was appropriate because of his interesting showmanship antics during his playing days.

I must interject at this point something that should have been said earlier, and that is the fact that Bill Schuster cannot be overlooked when it comes to Coast League buffoons. I would not be at all surprised if a majority of players who were in the League during Schuster's time would say without hesitation that he had no equal in this regard. My friend Paul Pettit sent along the following quote: *"Bill Schuster was one of the zaniest players in the PCL during the '40s."*

There were two reasons why I did not mention this man while on the subject of "characters." The first is that I was perhaps too young when Bill was at his best, thereby missing or not fully appreciating all his antics. I believe also that Bill was probably his funniest while pulling locker room shenanigans, which fans of course got very little info on. I can assure you, however, that I knew from the first time I saw him that he was a nut. I remember observing him one day at Wrigley Field during pre-game practice. He seemed to be having a ball. I thought to myself, "What is this guy cooking up for some unsuspecting teammate?"

Secondly, I did not mention Bill earlier because I wanted you to see first and foremost Bill Schuster, the baseball player, the man I personally consider the best shortstop in the PCL during my time. Why it didn't bother me to speak of Bobby Bragan as both a character and as an excellent manager and why it did bother me to speak of Bill Schuster as a clown but not as an excellent player, I absolutely can offer no reason, except to say that if you remember Schuster only as a funny man, then you've missed it. According to my calculations, Bill had a lifetime batting average of .277 and four times he finished second in fielding percentage among Coast League shortstops.

Now, after having openly stated my feelings, and only if you will promise to primarily remember Bill's exploits as a player, I'll give you two quick stories on him that took place during contests involving the Angels.

Bill related some fun he had at the expense of home plate umpire "Frisco" Edwards during a game at Portland. Frisco was a former catcher and his throwing hand showed the wear and tear that all receivers experience if they stay behind the plate for too many years. It came time for Schuster to come to bat, and he worked the pitcher for a walk. Edwards pointed to what he thought was first base, but his index finger was pointing right at second base. Bill, taking the umpire at his word, cut across the pitcher's box and went into second base. He was immediately tossed out of the game by a furious and sensitive Frisco Edwards.

The second incident Bill laughingly tells about took place in old Lane Field in San Diego. He came to bat and quickly grounded out. As he turned to head back toward the dugout, he caught some abuse from a bald-headed Padre fan in the first row of box seats. On a typical Schuster impulse, he abruptly stopped and kissed the fan right on his balding pate. Again, Bill was tossed out, this time for fraternizing with a fan. This story really grows on me. The more I reflect on it, the I more I lose my composure.

Yes, Bill's comical behavior was both impulsive and planned, and although I personally witnessed more of the Bragan and Johnson I humor, I admit that if a vote were taken Bill Schuster would probably be accorded the top honor among PCL players who engaged in the ludicrous.

Again, let me remind you that Bill Schuster was a super ballplayer. I am proud to have placed him on my PCL All-star Team.

Wow… I feel better after getting all of that off my chest!

### Kenny MINNIE MOUSE Sheehan

Sheehan was one of the smallest pitchers ever to see action in the PCL (5′ 7″). He had great difficulty with control throughout his Coast League days, which spanned five seasons. His last season of 1938 saw him win four games while losing 27. The name of "Minnie Mouse" was given him by his former manager, Lefty O'Doul.

### Arnold JIGGER Statz

In addition to his love for baseball, Jigger Statz was an avid golfer. An iron he used was called a jigger. Someone hung that name on him and it more than stuck. I don't know much about a jigger, but everyone knows *THE JIGGER!*

## Glen GABBY Stewart

The nickname of "Gabby" was hung on Glen Stewart for the reverse of what it should be. He was an extremely quiet man, a man of few words. I remember him very well during his Coast League days (he played several years for Hollywood). He seemed almost shy. I don't recall whether or not the nickname caused him to open up, but I would have to doubt it.

## Dick SOCKO Stuart

In contrast to Glen Stewart, Dick Stuart was a very loquacious individual. Stuart's bat was also talkative, particularly in the low minors. He did, or still does, hold the Western League record for home runs in one season (66). He accomplished this feat while playing at Lincoln, Nebraska. Hollywood announcer Mark Scott took a liking to Stuart and fully expected him to consistently rip home runs when he came to the Stars. In anticipation of this, Scott began calling him "Socko." As many of you know, Stuart not only had difficulty hitting home runs in two stints with Hollywood, but he had trouble making contact and really never made it as a member of the Stars. Stuart did get it together at Pittsburgh and Boston, giving those two teams many productive years.

## Ben VIRGIL Wade

Wade, for whatever reason, liked the name Virgil and called all his teammates by that name. As you might suspect, he in turn was referred to as Virgil.

## Kendall Cole CASEY Wise

Wise figured a way to get around using the name Kendall by combining the first letters of his first and second names. He always spelled it "Casey." I never remember him ever being referred to as Kendall. I wish I could say the same.

# THE CONTEST

As expected, Rich Timmis and I enjoyed the time spent pursuing our contest. Since the years spent in following PCL baseball were the most enjoyable in our baseball lives, we knew this ride down memory lane would be nothing short of super. We thoroughly discussed player's names as we worked our way through our respective lists. Pictures and autographs were examined in great detail. Even compiling the statistical data was fun. I knew all over again that we were a part of baseball at its very best.

Insofar as the outcome of the contest is concerned, we simply did not name a winner. The intent from the beginning was to recall and enjoy our baseball memories. Boy, did we do that! I can tell you that between us, we came out with an even 800 names from memory. A sample sheet similar to the ones we recorded names on follows on page 174. Also, an explanation as to the abbreviations on the contest forms is given.

I found out one thing, and that is the human mind (mine) is a strange thing. Let me explain. I listed a dozen or more names from memory of men who were fringe players to say the least. They were nonetheless right there, foremost in my mind, ready to put down on the contest sheets. Most of these of which I speak had only the proverbial cup of coffee in the Coast League. Now, since you know I what's coming, I'll admit it: I totally forgot some of the good and great players whose names immediately came back to me as soon as I saw them in print in my baseball guides. (These guides were used to prove, or disprove, our findings.)

I ask you, how could I fail to remember such "G" men as Johnny Gill, Marv Gudat and Dick Gyselman? I surely knew about them; they were PCL greats. I decided to blame my memory lapse on approaching senility.

> *Seattle Proprietor Emil Sick owned*
> *a healthy franchise.*

THE CHALLENGE

Attention:  Richard Timmis

Subject:  Pacific Coast League Name Calling Contest

Years Covering Contest:  1938-57

Sir:  You are hereby challenged by one Ken Stadler to a contest to
      determine who can name the most players, managers and coaches
      who performed in the Pacific Coast League.  Said players,
      managers and coaches must have performed sometime during the
      years 1938 through 1957.

Rules and Suggestions:  Each contestant will compile his list in
                        alphabetical order on the sheets provided and
                        must have said list completed on the date
                        which is mutually agreed upon.

When a contestant knows the position(s) and team(s) of the player, he
must so indicate.  A player's name will not, however, be eliminated
from the list because the contestants do not remember said player's
team and/or the position he played.  Infielders and outfielders may be
identified thus:  Inf-Out.  Their specific positions are not a part of
the contest.

A coach's name will be counted when both contestants agree that he did
in fact coach in the Pacific Coast League within the period of years
stipulated.  HOWEVER, if one contestant is certain his findings are
correct, and the other cannot positively dispute it -- IT WILL STAND!
This procedure is necessary because no mention of coaches is made on
the verification list obtained from the Baseball Hall of Fame.

It is agreed that if one contestant knows only the last name of a player
and the other contestant supplies the first name, the contestant sup-
plying the last name will receive credit toward his final count.  The
last name obviously carries more importance than the first.

It is agreed that if one contestant knows only the first name of a
player (unusual, uncommon first name) and the other supplies the last
name, said player's name will be added and counted on both lists, if
not already on the contestant's list who supplied the last name.

Each contestant is requested to bring the papers containing names of
players from which the final list was drawn.  Time will be allotted to
see if names have been omitted while copying them onto the permanent
sheets.  The omitted names must be shown to the other contestant.

No names may be added to either contestant's list from memory once the
contest begins.

It is suggested that each contestant add the names from the other's list
that they do not have on their own permanent sheet; this to be done on
a separate sheet(s) of paper as the contestants work their way through
the alphabet.  These names will not be added to the copying contestant's
permanent list, and thereby have no bearing on the outcome of the contest.

Each contestant should have an "uncertain list."  This list will contain
names of players the contestants are unsure of' and have therefore kept them
off the permanent lists.  Both contestants are expected to assist one
another in achieving a final determination of these names.

Contestants are urged to follow each and every hunch, whether a player,
manager, or coach, is eventually determined not to have performed during
the stipulated years, or at all.

A PLAYER'S NAME AND THE FACT THAT HE PLAYED IN THE PACIFIC COAST LEAGUE
BETWEEN THE YEARS OF 1938 and 1957 IS THE IMPORTANT ISSUE. The contestants
are expected to supply each other with team names and players' positions
without receiving credit.

Each contestant is urged to offer verbally, any information concerning listed
players which may be of interest. This to be done during the reading of
names, and should include interesting incidents which occurred during their
playing days, as well as matters of interest after their baseball careers
ended.

The specific year or years a person played, managed, or coached in the League
is not a part of the contest.

Several statistical sheets have been provided as a point of interest. Each
contestant has the right to carry statistical data to the extent he personally desires.

It is suggested that each contestant name a favorite player from his own
team and one favorite player from the remainder of League teams.

WINNER TO BE NAMED BY PLURALITY

THE CONTEST WILL START BY A COIN FLIP to determine who begins reading names
first. The winner of the toss will start by reading the names from his list
of uncertain players (this list to be compiled in alphabetical order). If it
is agreed that a player did indeed perform in the PCL during the stipulated
years, his name will be added to the permanent list of names. Upon comple-
tion of this, the other contestant will follow the same procedure. When this
is completed, the contestant who won the coin toss will begin the actual contest by reading the names of those whose last names begin with the letter "A."
The other contestant will then read his list from the same letter. From this
point on, the contestants will alternate through the alphabet.

A dinner will be held for both contestants at the Stadler home, after which
an interesting, exciting time of nostalgia will be had by the contestants.
The day of the dinner and date each list must be completed will be:

| 24 | April | 1982 |
|---|---|---|
| Day | Month | Year |

Coin toss won by Rich.

League teams from which to draw names:

Hollywood (Stars)          Sacramento (Solons)
Los Angeles (Angels)       San Diego (Padres)
Oakland (Oaks/Acorns)      San Francisco (Seals)
Portland (Beavers)         Seattle (Rainiers)
             Vancouver (Mounties)

AGREED AND HEREWITH SIGNED:

KEN STADLER, Contestant

RICHARD TIMMIS, Contestant

| B | 1 OF 3 | *PACIFIC COAST LEAGUE* | | | | | | | | |
|---|---|---|---|---|---|---|---|---|---|---|
| NAME | M/Co | P/C | INF | O.F. | TEAM (S) | | | | ADD. INFO | DEC |
| George Bamberger | | P | | | Oak | Van | | | X | |
| Dick Bartell | M | | | | Sac | | | | X | |
| Tony Bartirome | | | X | | Holly | | | | X | |
| Jim Baumer | | | X | | Holly | | | | X | |
| Dimitrios Baxes | | | X | | Holly | Port | LA | | N | |
| Gene Bearden | | P | | | SF | Oak | Sea | Sac | X | |
| Carlos Bernier | | | X | X | Holly | | | | X | |
| Steve Bilko | | | X | | LA | | | | X/N | X |
| Robert Blattner | | | X | | Sac | | | | X/N | |
| Bobby Bragan | M | C | | | Holly | | | | PIC X | |

The information listed on the above contest form shows various combinations which occurred in the contest.

## EXPLANATION OF ABBREVIATIONS
## ON CONTEST FORMS

M/Co – Manager/Coach

P/C – Pitcher/Catcher

Inf – Infielder

OF – Outfielder

Add Info – Additional Information:  N – Nickname

Pic – Picture

X – Something written about player

Dec – Deceased

# THE SPIRIT
# LIVES ON

Chris Goodchild is a young professional baseball player who began in the San Francisco Giants organization. He was the number one draft choice of the Giants several years back. After playing one season at Clinton, Iowa, and one year at Fresno, California, in Class-A ball, he went into the San Diego Padres organization at Reno, Nevada.

I met Chris and his lovely wife Diane through attendance at our church. We became good friends through periods of time spent in Bible study and through our mutual love for baseball. I have come to deeply care for this young couple.

I speak of Chris as we draw our nostalgic chat to a close because he is at that early stage in his career as were so many Coast Leaguers I remember in the past—that stage where the jury is still out and the future yet unknown. I speak of him because he represents those I remember in the PCL who became successful, and yes, all those who did not. And I speak of him because, even though he is at this writing in the low minors, he is nonetheless worthy of fan support and encouragement.

I remember standing near the dugout talking with Chris after a night game in Fresno when a young boy came up and asked for his autograph. Chris gave it to him, and then I told the boy to hold onto that piece of paper because he may just have gotten the signature of a future great major league pitcher. My heart went out to that youngster because he really cared about a player who represented his city and his team. My thoughts quickly went back across the years to when I was in the same position as that young lad with my team at Hollywood. They were my team. I couldn't care less about what classification they were in, or whether or not they had a winning record. From closely following Hollywood I went on to develop a deep love and respect for the entire League and for so many of its players. The fact that the League was outstanding was an added bonus.

*To Ken, Best wishes*
*Chris A Goodchild*

Baseball at all levels is relative. That is to say, the game is being played by people of equal ability. This means the sport is exciting and unpredictable wherever you see it played.

I'm glad for the Chris Goodchilds I saw play in years long since gone by, and for the great and illustrious history of the PCL.

Yes, it is true. Of all the minor leagues, none could challenge the Pacific Coast League where individual records are involved, be they seasonal or lifetime.

The following is a list of Pacific Coast League players, managers, coaches and umpires who have passed away. Insofar as I have been able to obtain these names, I want to pass them on to you.

**Cliff Aberson** – June 23, 1973 - Vallejo, California
**Emmett Ashford** (umpire) – March 1, 1980 - Marina del Rey, California
**Fred Baczewski** – November 14, 1976 - Culver City, California
**Win Ballou** – January 30, 1963 - San Francisco, California
**"Kewpie Dick" Barrett** – November 7, 1966 - Seattle, Washington
**John Bassler** – June 29, 1979 - Santa Monica, California
**Herm Besse** – August 13, 1972 - Los Angeles, California
**Hal Beven** – October 5, 1968 - New Orleans, Louisiana
**Steve Bilko** – March 7, 1978 - Wilkes Barre, Pennsylvania
**Hiram Bithorn** – January 1, 1952 - El Mante, Mexico
**Bill Brenzel** – June 12, 1979 - Oakland, California
**Tommy Bridges** – April 19, 1968 - Nashville, Tennessee
**Mickey Burnett** – Date and place of death unknown
**Cy Blanton** – September 13, 1945 - Norman, Oklahoma
**Rip Collins** – April 16, 1970 - New Haven, New York
**Dick Conger** – February 16, 1970 - Los Angeles, California
**Tod Davis** – December 31, 1978 - West Covina, California
**Frank Demeree** – August 30, 1958 - Los Angeles, California
**Charlie Dressen** – August 10, 1966 - Detroit, Michigan
**Karl Drews** – August 30, 1963 - Dania, Florida
**Walt Dubiel** – October 25, 1969 - Hartford, Connecticut
**Cedric Durst** – February 16, 1971 - San Diego, California
**Jimmy Dykes** – June 15, 1976 - Philadelphia, Pennsylvania
**Luke Easter** – Cleveland, Ohio
**Bob Elliott** – May 4, 1966 - San Diego, California
**Bill Englen** (umpire) – April 17, 1968 - Palo Alto, California
**Bob Fesler** – August 28, 1983 - Seattle, Washington
**Murray Franklin** – March 16, 1978 - Harbor City, California

**Sam Gibson** – Date and place of death unknown
**Joe Gordon** – March 14,1979 - Sacramento, California
**Herb Gorman** – April 5, 1953 - San Diego, California*
**Joe Grace** – September 18, 1969 - Murphysboro, Illinois
**Mickey Grasso** – October 15, 1975 - Miami, Florida
**Marv Gudat** – March 2, 1954 - Los Angeles, California
**Lee Handley** – April 8, 1970 - Pittsburgh, Pennsylvania
**Fred Haney** – November 9, 1977 - Beverly Hills, California
**Truck Hannah** – Spring, 1982 - Fountain Valley, California - Age 90
**Tommy Heath** – February 26, 1967 - Los Gatos, California
**Rollie Hemsley** – July 31, 1972 - Washington, D.C.
**Rogers Hornsby** – January 5, 1963 - Chicago, Illinois
**Joe Hoover** – September 2, 1965 - Los Angeles, California
**Fred Hutchinson** – November 12, 1964 - Bradenton, Florida
**Chet Johnson** – April 10, 1983 - Seattle, Washington
**Bob Joyce** – Date and place of death unknown
**Walt Judnich** – July 12, 1971 - Glendale, California
**Leo Kiely** – January 18, 1984 - Glen Ridge, N.J.
**Joe Krakauskas** – December 8, 1960 - Hamilton, Ontario, Canada
**Frank Kelleher** – April 13, 1979 - Stockton, California
**Ernie Lombardi** – September 26, 1977 - Santa Cruz, California
**Red Lynn** – October 27, 1977 - Bellville, Texas
**Al Lyons** – December 20, 1965 - Inglewood, California
**Harry Malmberg** – October 29, 1976 - San Francisco, California
**Gordon Maltzberger** – December 11, 1974 - Rialto, California
**Herschel Martin** – November 17, 1980 - Cuba, Missouri
**Pepper Martin** – March 5, 1965 - McAlester, Oklahoma
**Steve Mesner** – April 6, 1981 - San Diego, California
**Eddie Mulligan** – March 15, 1982 - San Raphael, California
**Heber Newsome** – December 15, 1968 - Ahoskie, North Carolina
**Ron Northey** – April 16, 1971 - Pittsburgh, Pennsylvania
**Lou Novikoff** – September 30, 1970 - South Gate, California
**Lefty O'Doul** – December 7, 1969 - San Francisco, California
**Bruggie Ogrodowski** – March 5, 1956 - San Francisco, California
**Don Osborn** – March 23, 1979 - Torrance, California
**Mel Ott** – November 21, 1958 - New Orleans, Louisiana

**Art Passarella** (umpire) – October 12, 1981 - Hemet, California
**Ken Penner** – May 28, 1959 - Sacramento, California
**Vic Picetti** – Date and place of death unknown
**Herm Pillette** – April 30, 1960 - Sacramento, California
**Marino Pieretti** – January 30, 1981 - San Francisco, California
**Cotton Pippen** – 1981
**Les Powers** – Date and place of death unknown
**Mel Queen** – April 4, 1982 - Fort Smith, Arkansas
**Whimpy Quinn** – September 1, 1954 - Los Angeles, California
**Willie Ramsdell** – October 8, 1969 - Wichita, Kansas
**Hal Rhyne, Sr.** – January 7, 1971 - Orangevale, California
**Hal Rhyne, Jr.** – August 5, 1978 - El Dorado Hills, California
**Charlie Root** – November 5, 1979 - Hollister, California
**Harry Ruby** – Date and place of death unknown
**Glen Russell** – September 26, 1976 - Los Angeles, California
**Jack Salveson** – December 28, 1974 - Norwalk, California
**Les Scarsella** – December 16, 1958 - San Francisco, California
**Merv Shea** – January 27, 1953 - Sacramento, California
**Kenny Sheehan** – March 6, 1982 - Berkeley, California
**Earl Sheely** – September 16, 1952 - Sacramento, California
**Vince Shupe** - April 5, 1962 - Canton, Ohio
**Harry Simpson** – Date and place of death unknown
**Bill Skiff** – December 25, 1976 - Bronxville, New York
**Mayo Smith** – November 24, 1977 - Boynton Beach, Florida
**Casey Stengel** – September 29, 1975 - Glendale, California
**Bill Sweeney** – April 18, 1957 - San Diego, California
**Jim Tabor** – August 22, 1953 - Sacramento, California
**Sal Taormina** – Date and place of death unknown
**Hollis Thurston** – September 14, 1973 - Los Angeles, California
**Jack Tobin** – January 18,1982 - Oakland, California
**Lou Tost** – February 22, 1967 - Santa Clara, California
**Oscar Vitt** – January 31, 1963 - Oakland, California
**Eddie Waitkus** – September 15, 1972 - Boston, Massachusetts
**Lon Warneke** (umpire) – June 23, 1976 - Hot Springs, Arkansas
**George "Pinky" Woods** – October 30, 1982 - Los Angeles, California
**E. H. Zwilling** – La Crescenta, California

*Died of a heart attack on the field during game, Lane Field

## REFERENCE MATERIAL

*Reach/Spaulding Official Baseball Guide.* Cooperstown, N.Y.: National Baseball Hall of Fame and Museum, Inc., 1938–1957

*Who's Who in Baseball.* New York: Who's Who in Baseball Magazine Co., Inc., 1950, 1952, 1955

Obojski, Robert. *Bush League.* New York: Macmillan Publishing Co., Inc., 1975

Smalling, R.J., and Eckes, Dennis W. *Baseball Address List.* Laurel, Md.: Den's Collectors Den, 1980

Society for American Baseball Research. *Minor League Baseball Stars.* Cooperstown, NY: SABR, 1978

*Rollie Truitt's Scrapbook, 7th Edition.* Portland, Ore.: Portland Beavers, 1954

*Official Program.* All-Pacific Recreation Fund, Inc. Baseball game, 1944

## CONTACTING THE AUTHOR

We welcome your comments on how well you enjoyed (or not) this book, to help us to make it even better in future editions. Please visit the official web page for *Pacific Coast League – One Man's Memories* at **www.MarbekPublications.com/PCL** where you can find my contact information, any updates or errata notes, and feel free to leave your own personal recollections, rants and raves as a fellow fan of great baseball and the great years of the Pacific Coast League.